Buzzards to Bluebirds

Improve Your Child's Learning & Behavior In Six Weeks

Help Stop LD, ADD, ADHD, Dyslexia, School Dropouts & School Failures

Allen & Virginia Crane

Original art by Deanna Christensen and Cindy Howard.

Cover and internal design by P. Dooley Graphics, Gulph Mills, PA.

Edited and produced by the Writing Team, H. R. Dawkins, Managing Editor.

Library of Congress Cataloging-in-Publication

Crane, Allen and Virginia, P.O. Box 242, Wray, CO. 80758.

Buzzards to Bluebirds
Improve Your Child's Learning & Behavior
In Six Weeks

1. Non-fiction

- parents and teachers guide to helping students
- how to test and train students to improve learning & behavior
- a manual for testing and training vision
- a guide for resolving health problems

ISBN 0-943599-87-3

First Edition

Contents

Authors' Preface

There are so many people to whom the authors owe so much. While working as elementary counselors in Farmington, New Mexico, first grade teacher Mrs. Winters would meet Allen at the door every day demanding to know why Sheila could not learn to read. He kept telling her the child had failed the Bender Gestalt Perception test. Mrs. Winters would ask, "What do we do about it?" "I don't know," was the reply. While reading everything he could get his hands on, Allen learned that Dr. Howard Walton, an optometrist in Culver City, California, could correct vision perception problems. After flying to Culver City and talking to Dr. Walton one weekend, Allen had an answer for Mrs. Winters the next Monday. Sheila's problems were corrected in six weeks, and she did learn to read. (Dr. Walton had told Allen about the perception program developed by the Winter Haven Lions Club Foundation Program in Winter Haven, Florida.)

The authors attended a summer session on Orton Society's multisensory approach taught by Arlene Sonday. In using this approach, children hear a word, see the word and trace it with their fingers all at the same time. For children with learning problems, this is often a good approach.

While the Cranes were team-teaching Sioux children in Pine Ridge, South Dakota, Herbie came into their lives. This boy copied poorly from the chalkboard even though he wore new glasses which corrected his eyesight to 20/20. The Cranes traveled over 20,000 miles that summer trying to learn why Herbie couldn't copy from the chalkboard. Their first stop was the Lions Club in Winter Haven, Florida, where they met Dr. Charles McQuarrie. That club had sponsored over twenty-five years of research in perception. What a great program and information source. Note: this information is now in the library of the Optometric Extension Program Foundation (OEP) in Santa Ana, California; see Resources in the back for the address.

Then the authors went on to the University of Houston School of Optometry, where they visited for a week with Dr. Gordon McKee. They observed indepth vision screening and vision training programs which were being conducted in public schools. They visited with Dr. Arthur Seiderman in Elkins Park, Pennsylvania, to learn about his approach to vision problems in schools. At Southern California College of Optometry in Fullerton, California, they talked again to Dr. Howard Walton and conferred with Doctors John Griffin, Michael Rouse and Julie Ryan.

Everywhere, they kept hearing about one optometrist, Bruce Wick O.D. Ph.D., of Rapid City, South Dakota. Finally, they did talk with Dr. Wick, who came to Pine Ridge and screened over 420 elementary students. This dedicated specialist went to the teachers armed with the results of his tests and described the classroom and playground behavior of each child. Teachers were so impressed that it was arranged for the authors to do vision training activities with 90 children for 9 weeks. Dr. Wick visited every other week to schedule appropriate activities. The academic improvement was great, but the biggest change was playground behavior, which became nearly hassle-free.

Allen went to a 3-day hands-on functional vision workshop for optometrists by Dr. William Ludlum in Hillsboro, Oregon. Dianna Ludlum, his wife, had worked as a resource teacher and psychologist in schools. Both Ludlums were really helpful.

The authors visited for two weeks at the State University of New York College of Optometry. Most of their time was spent in the library. Between classes they visited with Doctors Nathan Flax, Irwin Suchoff, Harold Solan and Martin Birnbaum. What a superb experience, a fine library and a wealth of knowledge. Information the Cranes thought they were discovering had been published decades earlier.

For almost a decade, the Cranes tried to replicate for other districts the vision screening and vision training activities program they had at Pine Ridge, South Dakota. They could not. When he realized the work was not receiving the quality of optometric evaluation Dr. Wick had given on the earlier project, Allen persuaded Dr. Wick to put his testing knowledge on computer. The first school in which the Cranes worked with this computer program was the Rock Springs Catholic Elementary School in Rock Springs, Wyoming, where Mrs. Tracy Zuehlsdorff was principal.

Allen asked Dr. William Ludlum to recommend a good optometrist in Wyoming or Colorado to help with a research project. The recommendation was Dr. Roger Dowis in Boulder, Colorado. Under the direction of Dr. Dowis, Allen worked at Nederland Elementary School, Nederland, Colorado, where Don Hanson was principal. About 350 students were screened and vision training activities were accomplished with about 100 children. While working on this project, Allen realized tests to evaluate the results did not exist. There were vision tests and there were reading tests, but there were no tests to evaluate children's functional vision as they read for a realistic amount of time.

Mr. Crane designed the Performance-based Vision Stress Test (PVS Test, initially called the Crane-Wick Vision and Hearing Efficiency Test) at Nederland to evaluate results. Subsequently, he normed (established exactly how much visual work a child can complete at each grade level) this test on over 2,000 children in six states.

The PVS Test was first given to 170 students at Bayfield Elementary and Middle School, Bayfield, Colorado, where Don Magill was principal. Dr. Jay Highland and the school nurse used a modified New York State Optometric Association Vision Screening Test to do school vision screening at the same time, so Allen could compare results of the PVS Test with their results. The PVS Test agreed with their screening on 121 students. Forty-five students failed this test but passed the other screening; 31 of these 45 developed symptoms (headaches, blurry vision and so forth) when doing the test. Only four students who failed the school screening passed the PVS Test. None of these four developed symptoms. It is possible that these students may have been suppressing the vision in one eye.

The authors had a Federal VI-B grant at the Saratoga Elementary School in Saratoga, Wyoming, to evaluate and correct functional vision problems. Jeff Deggenhart was principal. The vision screening and vision training activities were under the direction of Doctors Jim Spicer of Saratoga and Alvin Alberts of Cheyenne, Wyoming. There the authors learned about vertical alignment when they screened over 259 students and did visual activities with about 129 students. About a third of those students still developed symptoms when the project ended. After retesting the children with symptoms, it was evident most of those had problems of vertical alignment. At the beginning of the project, the authors had assumed that glasses would be used to correct vertical alignment problems. They discovered most vision specialists do not even test for vertical alignment. They did vertical visual activities with the students to whom they had access, and in two to three weeks the youngsters were symptom-free. The job is not done until the symptoms are gone.

Mr. Crane went back to the Rock Springs Catholic Elementary School in Rock Springs, Wyoming, and applied the new knowledge he had gained. A red-headed, blue-eyed second grader changed Allen's life when she said, "Mister Crane, will you fix my eyes so I don't get headaches when I read?" Thanks to Dr. Richard Canestrini, this was accomplished. This student's eyes had been checked twice by a "vision" specialist that year. She had been told she had "perfect 20/20 vision." She did have 20/20 sight, but her eye alignment, focusing and eye movement were all poor.

Whenever a student did not make significant weekly gains, Dr. Canestrini told Mr. Crane what changes to make in therapy. Parents became involved in all phases of the program: screening, vision training activities and record keeping. Of the 102 students tested, 81 brought back permission for 10 minutes a day of vision training activities for four weeks. Seven students graduated from the program in two weeks, another 32 in three weeks. After the fourth week only 12 students of the original 81 still needed vision training activities. Of these 12 students, 7 had been referred to vision specialists for being farsighted or nearsighted and only 3 of the 12 still reported symptoms.

Other practitioners who have been a great help include Doctors Sue Lowe of Laramie, Wyoming, Frank Puckett of Colorado Springs, Colorado, Mike English of Farmington, New Mexico, and Stan Kaseno of San Bernadino, California, all of whom are optometrists whose specialty practices focus on behavioral work. Whenever a child was tested who was not making significant gains, these practitioners always came through. They always returned phone calls. Thanks.

Bob Williams, Executive Director of the Optometric Extension Program Foundation (OEP), has been a great resource. The OEP Foundation provides continuing education in functional vision problems. Mr. Williams and OEP Foundation staff have always been available to discuss questions and refer the authors to people and helpful resources.

Jonnie Kennedy, a fantastic librarian in Green River, Wyoming, told the Cranes about *Smart But Feeling Dumb* by Harold N. Levinson, M.D. (see Resources in the back). Other causes besides vision can trigger learning problems.

Allen's brother Robert Crane sent him *Total Concentration*, another book by Dr. Harold N. Levinson and *Solving the Puzzle of Your Hard-To-Raise Child* by William G. Crook, M.D. and Laura Stevens. *In Bad Taste: The MSG Syndrome* by George R. Schwartz, M.D., and *Excitotoxins: The Taste that Kills* by Russell L. Blaylock, M.D.

Most of all, John A. Thomas, O.D., of Denver, Colorado, and Bruce Wick, O.D., Ph.D., of Houston, Texas, patiently shared their knowledge and answered endless questions. For well over a decade, phone bills were never less than $300 a month.

It is the sincere hope of the authors that they have not left unmentioned anyone who helped in the development of their skills or knowledge.

How to Use This Book

The first part of this book is for parents of children who are having difficulties in school. It is written especially for those whose children have been labeled learning disabled (LD), dyslexic or attention deficit disordered (ADD), attention deficit hyperactive disordered (ADHD), emotionally disturbed, hyperactive, loud and so on. It is also for those whose children have a short attention span, whom the school wishes to retain, who are not working up to their full potential or who are at high risk of dropping out of school. It is written as well for parents and students who do not read for pleasure.

This book outlines exactly how you can help your child realize his or her potential in a matter of weeks. You can help children transform themselves—from buzzards to bluebirds.

Problems that cause difficulties in school can range from mild to severe. While norming (establishing exactly how much visual work a child can complete at each grade level) the Performance-based Vision Stress Test (PVS Test), Allan Crane was introduced to many youngsters, including Jessica, valedictorian of her senior class; her difficulties were mild: headaches after reading or doing school work for only ten minutes. She read so slowly it took her an hour to read what other students completed in fifteen minutes. Others, Rickie and Tony, are children whose situations were severe and well documented.

Rickie was diagnosed schizophrenic and spent years in institutions, receiving the very best "medicine" could offer. Rickie's problems were neither accurately diagnosed nor corrected until her father, a highly respected psychiatrist, started making decisions for Rickie rather than relying on "experts." When her functional vision difficulties and nutrition problems were corrected, she was able to live a normal life. Rickie and her father co-authored the book *Rickie.*[1]

Tony's parents did not believe the diagnostic team (which consisted of a child developmental specialist, speech and language therapists, a physical therapist and a pediatrician) when their son was diagnosed as autistic and severely mentally retarded. The team reported it was doubtful Tony would ever talk; also, they noted he would always need someone to take care of him.[2] Actually, Tony was a very intelligent boy. An undetected, severe allergy to milk was affecting his brain and totally negating his ability to go through normal early childhood development. When cow's milk was removed from Tony's diet (he was then 2 ½), his younger sister, who insisted Tony do everything that she did, took him through the stages of development Tony had missed. Mary Callahan wrote her son's story in the book *Fighting for Tony.*[3]

Mary Callahan points out that parents of handicapped children are nine times more likely to divorce than the general population.[4] In many cases not only are families struggling daily to live with and help their child, they are also facing stresses in their marriage.

Vision and medical problems are often inherited; with this book, family members can gain insight into their own difficulties *and* those of a child and find possible solutions. ***It's never too late*** to correct problems. Those of adults may include:

difficulty concentrating;
trouble keeping a job;
poor comprehension of written material;

not reading for pleasure;
avoiding jobs that need paperwork;
not liking to drive at night;
memories of having problems in school.

The second part of the book has sections written for teachers and other professionals who work with children. **By using what is outlined in this book, over half of *all* children in any classroom can be helped.** Many top students will become more efficient, read for pleasure and will no longer have symptoms such as headaches or blurry vision. Many average and slower students will go from making low or failing grades to passing and high grades. They will be free of symptoms and read for pleasure.

Most learning, attention and behavioral problems are caused by medical or vision problems—or a combination of these—and can be treated and corrected in a matter of weeks. If a child's problems are severe, the resolution may take much longer. Pieces of the puzzle are available to parents, teachers and doctors who work together. You can watch your real child emerge.

Part I
For Parents

Where Does a Parent Begin?

Your child is not doing as well in school as you believe he or she could. The school calls to say your child is having problems in the classroom. Possibly, you have been told your child should be trying harder or that your child could do the work if he just would. Your child reads slowly and does not remember what was read. The child is often noisy, hyperactive, irritable, clumsy or has a short attention span. The school has labeled the child a problem or attention deficit disordered, attention deficit hyperactive disordered, learning disabled, dyslexic, behavior disordered or emotionally disturbed. Alternatively, perhaps, you are providing home schooling and feel that your child is not making good progress.

What can you as a parent do to ensure that your child receives the necessary help? Educational success is vital. Success as an adult is built upon a foundation of good education. How far can your child go in school? Attitudes toward adults and authority, as well as self confidence and self respect, will be affected during the early years. Will full potential be realized? Where do you begin looking for answers?

Performance-based Observation & Testing

The first thing you must do is determine whether the problem is medical or vision or a combination of both.

You say your child was just checked by an optometrist, ophthalmologist, family doctor, pediatrician and/or school nurse and the problem could not be a vision or medical problem!

The key to deciding if the difficulty is a medical or a vision problem is *performance-based testing.* You need to know how your child actually performs when doing school work for one hour to several hours and over several weeks. Does the child receive As on spelling tests but leave out obvious sounds in words not on the list? Does your child have good and bad days or times of the day that are better than others? Are these related to certain foods or particular locations or times of the year? What happens to the child's eyes while s/he reads for 30 minutes? Is the image seen at the beginning of the task clear and stable or does the image blur and/or seem to move, swim, overlap or vary in any way? Does the child get a headache after a few minutes? Does your child have trouble looking back and forth quickly and efficiently when copying from the chalkboard?

Medical doctors must rely on information they are given about school performance. Most do not see their patients performing school-type tasks even for a few minutes. Vision tests given by optometrists, ophthalmologists, family doctors and school nurses are not sufficiently related to school tasks. Unlike the daily demands of school, each vision test is over in a matter of seconds. "Instantaneous testing" is the rule in doctors' offices, especially vision testing, and it fails to find the more subtle functional problems that are devastating to a child.

The rationale for *Performance-based Observations* is similar to that of cardiologists giving the treadmill stress test as a person walks about 5 miles per hour up a 10-12 percent incline for about 15 minutes. Numerous quick (instantaneous) tests run on the heart cannot tell the doctor what is learned from a treadmill stress test. The stress test tells the cardiologist how the heart is functioning in real life situations. Sustained, performance-based testing tells how the visual system functions in real-life school situations such as reading, taking notes and doing homework.

Optometrists, ophthalmologists and school nurses normally perform a few tests that take a minimum amount of time and consequently fail to diagnose functional vision problems. Medical doctors do not recognize the educational symptoms listed on the form above as allergy related.[5, 6] Medical doctors do blood tests and traditional allergy testing and rely on secondhand information about symptoms and behaviors and how the child does school work; as a consequence, the professionals may fail to diagnose some medical problems.

The following sections explain observations you can use to determine whether your child needs to visit a vision specialist, a medical doctor or both.

Performance-based Observation of Your Child: Vision

You have three ways to evaluate your child's functional vision skills.

(1) You can listen to and observe your child reading for 30 minutes; (2) Ask your child's teacher to fill out OEP Foundation's *Educator's Guide to Classroom Vision Problems* (see p. 46) from observations of classroom performance; or (3) You can give the Performance-based Vision Stress (PVS) Test. All three are described in this book.

Option 1: Listen To Child Read

Listen to your child read for 30 minutes and observe reading behaviors. Note on the Performance-based Vision and Medical Checklist if your child gets too close to the book, tilts his head, covers one eye, loses his place or uses a finger to keep his place, reads very slowly, skips two letter words or reads three letter words backwards (saw-was), has to go to the bathroom or get a drink while reading (avoidance behavior). These are signs of a visual problem.

After the reading is finished ask your child how s/he feels and how the letters looked, then question your child about what was just read. Record answers under **Symptoms reported after reading** (p. 5)

The problem is vision-related if you receive any of these answers:

my head hurts;
my eyes burn or hurt;
the print is blurry;
the words swim or wiggle;
I feel dizzy or weird;
I feel tired or sleepy.

If your child has trouble understanding the story or has to re-read portions of the story in order to tell you what was read, you have identified even more clues to a vision related problem. **Record this as poor comprehension.**

By January, first graders should be able to read 80 words per minute silently, fourth graders 158 words per minute, eighth graders 204 words per minute and twelfth graders 250 words per minute with good comprehension.[7] For a full listing of grade level/words per minute, see the chart on p. 32. You can figure how many words are read per minute by having your child read **silently** for one minute and counting the words read. You need to ask questions about the story to be sure it is understood. Even when all visual systems are functioning properly, few can compete successfully in the classroom if they mentally say every word read. **Write these on the vision observations list.**

Ask what activities your child cannot do as fast or as long as other students in the class. If these activities include copying from the chalkboard or reading, you have yet another proof of vision problems. Does your child ever read for pleasure? If not, this is a further indication of a vision problem. **Record these observations on the list.**

Performance-based Vision and Medical Checklist

Name ____________________________________
Age ______________ Birthday ____________

Vision observations:

- ☐ Gets close to work
- ☐ Uses finger to keep place
- ☐ Tilts head
- ☐ Covers one eye
- ☐ Loses his place
- ☐ Reads very slowly
- ☐ Reads choppily
- ☐ Skips two letter words
- ☐ Reads words backwards (was-saw)
- ☐ Eyes red or watery
- ☐ Rubs eyes
- ☐ Has to get a drink
- ☐ Has to go the bathroom
- ☐ Reads _____ words per minute

Symptoms reported after reading:

- ☐ Head hurts
- ☐ Eyes hurt or burn
- ☐ Print blurry
- ☐ Words swim or wiggle
- ☐ Feels dizzy or weird
- ☐ Feels tired or sleepy
- ☐ Poor comprehension
- ☐ Comprehension decreases the longer the child reads

Other______________________________________

Indications of medical problems related to education:

- ☐ Does not turn in assignments
- ☐ Reverses letters (b-d, h-y,) when writing
- ____ Short attention span
- ____ Hyperactive
- ☐ Leaves out obvious sounds-spelling
- ☐ Has poor handwriting
- ☐ Louder than other children
- ☐ Irritable
- ☐ Clumsy
- ☐ Good Days and Bad Days

Performance-based Vision Stress Test

% efficiency

- ____ Near-Far Copying
- ____ Saccadic eye movement
- ____ Prolonged eye Teaming
- ____ Y/N Fatigue Factor

Symptoms ___________________________________
____

Medical-Allergy Symptoms

(May or may not be present)

- ☐ Has had extensive antibiotics

Skin

- ☐ itching
- ☐ burning
- ☐ flushing
- ☐ rash
- ☐ coldness
- ☐ hives
- ☐ blisters
- ☐ red spots

Throat

- ☐ sore
- ☐ dry
- ☐ tickling
- ☐ clearing
- ☐ hoarseness
- ☐ hacking cough
- ☐ tongue coated

Nervous System

- ☐ headache
- ☐ drowsy
- ☐ slow
- ☐ irritable
- ☐ depressed
- ☐ overactive
- ☐ crying
- ☐ jittery
- ☐ abdominal pain
- ☐ muscle ache
- ☐ bed wetting
- ☐ drooling

Ears

- ☐ red lobes
- ☐ earache
- ☐ dizziness
- ☐ fullness
- ☐ ringing

Eyes

- ☐ red
- ☐ itchy
- ☐ watery
- ☐ dark circles
- ☐ wrinkles (under)

Nose

- ☐ red
- ☐ runny nose
- ☐ sneezing
- ☐ nasal itching
- ☐ many symptoms started after antibiotics began

A small percentage of children will say they can read for a long time and can do it faster than others but actually are very slow and read only about ten minutes before stopping to go to the bathroom or to get a drink. If in doubt, ask the teacher if your child is behaving in this manner.

Option 2: Educator's Guide and Checklist to Classroom Vision Problems

This pamphlet by the OEP Foundation is a valuable document. Teachers see students perform four or five hours a day and can make excellent observations. Teachers are concerned about their students and many are happy to record their observations. Others have such a heavy class load that they do not have time. As is true with Options 1 and 3, the Educator's Guide is effective only when used in conjunction with the Screen Your Vision Specialist Form. Both are in the Resources section and may be copied.

Option 3: Performance-based Vision Stress Test

For exact, standardized and normed evaluation of functional vision efficiency, give the Performance-based Vision (PVS) Test Dr. Bruce Wick and the authors developed and normed in 1987. The PVS Test indicates exactly how many numbers or letters an efficient child is able to copy in 1 minute from 20 feet and how many lines of work the child is able to "read" in 15 minutes without developing symptoms. This test was normed on children in kindergarten through twelfth grade. The only knowledge necessary to take this test is numbers to five or the alphabet. See p. 49 for more details and how to give the test. **Record the results on the Performance-based Vision and Medical Checklist.**

If in doubt, use all three options and compare the results.

Performance-based Observation Of Your Child: Medical

Give 20 spelling words from the Crane Word List (p. 48) at your child's grade level to see if obvious sounds in words are left out. For example, the child leaves out the b in table. If obvious sounds in three words in the list are left out, there is a medical problem. **Record results of spelling the 20 words under Indications of medical problems related to education (p. 5).**

A medical problem is indicated when your child has one or more of the following performance-based problems:

not turning in assignments;

leaves out obvious sounds when writing or reading words;

has poor handwriting;

reverses letters (b-d, h-y, m-w, p-g, p-b) when writing;

is louder than other children;

is irritable;

is clumsy;

is hyperactive with a short attention span;

has good days and bad days.

Record observations under Indications of medical problems related to education (p. 5).

Dr. Rapp uses handwriting in diagnosing allergies and determining effective treatment.

Samples can be seen in Dr. Doris Rapp's book and video.[8, 9]

From these observations you can tell if your child needs to see a vision specialist or a medical doctor, or both. You should be able to obtain the help you need.

The Whole Child

A word of caution: teamwork among the healing professions has not been a hallmark of their work with children. Allergists have concentrated upon identifying allergies and treating them. Psychologists have focused upon psychological problems. Vision specialists have tested eyes and prescribed glasses. Hearing specialists, speech therapists, pediatricians have looked at children and their problems from the perspective of their profession or, perhaps on rare occasions, in conjunction with one other profession. No one is looking at the whole child. **You, the parent, must look at the whole child.**

Rickie saw more than fifteen specialists, all of whom thought their particular specialty was "the answer" to resolving her problems.[10] Yet Rickie spent over ten years in mental hospitals and received everything from shock therapy, psychotherapy, and medication to isolation treatment. Her father was a leading psychiatrist. Many of the specialists consulted were leaders in their fields. Once her nutrition and vision problems were corrected, she was able to lead a normal life. Rickie had 20/30 vision acuity in each eye on the regular eye exam; yet when under visual stress she became legally blind. We don't realize we do not have models to tell us how to see. Rickie's comment was, "Doesn't everyone see this way?"[11]

Until children with problems receive proper help, it is likely they will be given many incorrect labels, among them: learning disabled, short attention span, hyperactive, lazy, visual dyslexic, auditory dyslexic, attention deficit disordered, attention deficit hyperactive disordered and emotionally disturbed.[12, 13, 14, 15, 16] Schools often place these children in special education classes; physicians and psychiatrists treat the symptoms with medication; counselors and psychologists talk to the child. If the child has a vision problem or medical problem, such activities only hide the problem. Think of it as putting a bandaid on a splinter. The bandaid will protect the end of the splinter, thus stopping some pain, but the problem still exists and will persist.

From your observations, the teacher's observations and/or the PVS Test, you will have an idea whether your child's problems are mostly visual or medical or seem to be a combination of the two. The appropriate sections to help you deal with your child's problems are p. 7 for vision problems and p. 19 for medical problems.

Vision Problems

You have determined that your child has vision problems. You did this by observing your child performing a visual activity (reading for thirty minutes, having the teacher complete the vision checklist, and/or giving the PVS test). These activities all evaluate functional vision and are not what are generally found in vision exams or screenings. Most vision screenings and exams take place in an extremely short time and cannot truly determine how a person functions in the real world of school or workplace, where the eyes must carry on sustained activity.

School vision screening is no exception. Not only are screenings instantaneous, often they do not test vision at reading distance. This is true of the Snellen Chart which is the most widely used screening in many schools and in family doctors' and pediatricians' offices. The Snellen Chart, the big E wall chart, was designed over one hundred years ago at about the time buffalo hunting was in full swing. It was a good test back then to tell you if you had adequate eyesight to hunt buffalo (provided the buffalo was standing in dead grass, twenty feet away and not moving). If you expect your child to learn to read, it is suggested that the Snellen Chart is not a good place with which to start the analysis of the vision system. Many experts in the vision field are trying to eliminate the use of the Snellen Chart.

Approximately 12 percent of the vision specialists test for functional vision problems as noted by H. R. Dawkins in *The Suddenly Successful Student.*[17] This concise paperback, which is available from the OEP Foundation, offers an overview of behavioral optometry. Most vision examinations conducted by optometrists and ophthalmologists are instantaneous tests and are not based on how children perform in classroom settings. Even though many vision specialists have had courses in giving tests to identify functional vision problems, they are not required to give these tests in actual examinations; most do not. This may be partially because training programs have a heavy emphasis on pathology (disease, infection and injury of the eye), and surgical specialties; this leaves little time to emphasize functional care, which is considered less glamorous and less profitable.

In 1987, Dr. Bruce Wick and Allen Crane developed and published the Crane-Wick Vision and Hearing Efficiency Test, now the Performance-based Vision Stress Test.[18] This test was given to over 2,000 students in six states to establish how much work a child with efficient vision can do. See p. 49 for a description of the test. The test evaluates vision skills necessary for school success without the student having to read words or comprehend. It is based on how many lines of visual work a student can do in 15 minutes and how many numbers or letters can be copied in 1 minute from a distance of 20 feet.

When the PVS Test was normed, 53-56 percent of the students developed headaches, blurry vision, dizziness, got closer than 8 inches from their work or developed other severe symptoms after only 30 minutes of school-related visual activity. When these students were referred to vision specialists, reports usually came back "20/20 eyesight and everything normal." Parents were angry about wasting money for a vision exam when "nothing was wrong." However, if you look at the eye exams most of these students received from the vision specialist, the student had received a test that evaluated only one or two parts of their visual system and had spent less than 10 minutes with the vision specialist.

If a student develops symptoms while performing a vision task which is similar to a normal classroom activity, there is a vision problem.[19] It is not acceptable to develop symptoms while reading or copying for a few minutes. This serves to illustrate that most optometrists and ophthalmologists commonly overlook vision problems severe enough to cause learning, behavioral and emotional difficulties.

The only functional vision problem the PVS Test does not detect is suppression of the vision of one eye.[20] A child who has had eye surgery for crossed eyes often uses only one eye. Two simple tests easily verify this. One is the Brock String activity described on p. 14. The other is red/green glasses and a red/green reading bar (see Resources, p. 42). The red/green reading bar is placed over a page of print. When the child puts on the red/green glasses and reads, the eye behind the red lens reads through the red strip and the eye behind the green lens reads through the green strip. Individuals who are using only one eye can read only half of the print. Both tests need to be performed because suppression can be present under different conditions of stress and distance.

Optometrist or Ophthalmologist?

The emphasis of ophthalmology is eye disease and eye surgery; this is their domain, the area of expertise. Dr. Malcolm L. Mazow, an ophthalmologist, wrote in the discussion section of his paper "Acute Accommodative and Convergence Insufficiency,"[21] "My impression is that many ophthalmologists handle this disorder poorly and many of the patients end up under the care of optometrists." Dr. David L. Guyton in the same discussion said, "I agree with Dr. Mazow...we have probably abdicated the study of accommodation and convergence to the optometric profession. A perusal of the literature will reveal that most of the advances in this area are being made in the optometric institutions by vision scientists who use definitions and terms with which we are not even familiar."

All optometrists are thoroughly trained to detect eye disease, examine binocular vision and perform refraction (fitting glasses). Beyond that, in postdoctoral study, optometrists learn one or more specialties that interest them. Some specialize in contact lenses, some in geriatrics, some in functional vision, some in sports vision. The specialty of behavioral optometry is for individuals who have developmental or functional vision problems. One of the chief purposes of the OEP Foundation (founded in the 1930s) is to provide optometrists with continuing education on the treatment of functional vision problems.

When unable to detect a vision problem quickly, the non-behavioral vision specialists may suggest that your child be referred to a psychologist or psychiatrist to explain your child's symptoms. Remember that if your child develops symptoms while reading, **it is a vision problem** and does not require a psychologist or psychiatrist. Be sure to screen vision specialists to find an optometrist who will do the testing you require and give the assistance you need to correct any vision problems discovered. Medical problems such as thyroid imbalance and glaucoma can cause vision problems. Optometrists who give complete functional vision exams are also trained to examine for these problems and make necessary referrals to appropriate care providers.

The authors believe the most overlooked problem in vision is vertical mis-alignment: one eye aims higher than the other eye; technically termed hyper- or hypophoria or tropia. The established allowable norm used by many eye doctors is two diopters (a unit that expresses the power of a lens).[22] This means that one eye may normally aim about ¼ inch lower at reading distance than the other eye. Many behavioral optometrists use ½ diopter as the allowable norm.

If words looked like this,
would reading be fun? Would
you have to rest your eyes?

Sample of the difference ½ diopter can make.

In some cases, ¼ of a diopter can prevent a child from learning the alphabet and reading properly because of all the extra effort required to keep a clear image. The child can do this for only a short period of time and comprehension will be poor. The eyes can keep good alignment only for a short time and then must be rested. This can explain why many children are labeled as having a short attention span, being hyperactive or having an attention deficit hyperactive disorder. Actually, many are resting their eyes, an involuntary physical need. A vertical alignment problem is easier to correct than diagnose. During our research, we found only a few behavioral optometrists diagnose and correct vertical problems directly. Many behavioral optometrists depend on vertical problems to self-correct while other vision problems are being corrected.

In our experience, directly training vertical alignment at the beginning of training activities shortens the total time required to eliminate visual symptoms. If the vertical alignment is left to correct itself, it may lengthen vision training to months or even years. By correcting the vertical problem directly and simultaneously with other vision problems, the time required for vision training is reduced.

Note that a behavioral optometrist may correct vertical alignment problems by including the proper amount of prism in glasses to compensate for the problem. These doctors use several methods to determine the prism correction necessary. One technique is patching one eye for up to forty-eight hours, then remeasuring the vertical alignment. A second technique is a fixation disparity test which takes special equipment and about twenty minutes.[23] A series of prisms is used and a vertical alignment curve plotted to determine the amount of prism needed. Other methods are sometimes used.[24] These work very well as long as a person continues to receive lenses from a doctor who puts vertical prisms in the lenses. The problem remains, however, and will show up again if the lenses are prescribed by a doctor who does not do this.

If your child uses a finger to keep his place, covers one eye, tilts his head, or frequently loses his place when reading, insist on doing vertical alignment activities. By doing these activities three minutes a day, most vertical alignment problems can be corrected in four weeks or less. You will find in the back of this book, in Resources, a list of organizations to help you locate a vision specialist in your area who works with patients with functional vision problems.

Professionals belonging to the organizations listed in Resources may only have registered with the group because of an interest in learning about behavioral optometry or functional vision. In order to locate someone who has the competence and knowledge to help you, ask for a list of Diplomates from the Section of Binocular Vision and Perception of the American Academy of Optometry or a list of Fellows of the College of Optometrists in Visual Development.

These professionals have passed extensive written and oral examinations by certification boards in behavioral optometry. If none is in your community, call a Diplomate or Fellow listed for the location of the most qualified person in your area. Note that even Fellows and Diplomates may not correct vertical mis-alignment and you may have to insist on your child doing the activities on page 18. Some optometrists do not join any of the professional organizations but have the necessary knowledge and training and provide good care in functional vision. If you think you have one of these doctors in your community, the form Screen Your Optometrist, p. 11, will help you with your decision.

Children's eyes and vision systems change rapidly. However, any activity, whether walking or learning baseball, takes time and practice – it is the same for vision; children need to be checked at least once a year by a vision specialist who offers diagnosis and prescribes any necessary treatment. **It is up to you, as a parent, to locate the optometrist best prepared to test your child's functional vision.** Although glasses are necessary for many children, our research shows that glasses alone will only totally correct the problems of about 12 percent of the children. Vision training activities will be necessary to relieve the other children of symptoms. (See p. 12 for necessary vision training activities.)

Many vision specialists usually perform only a few tests to prescribe lenses and do not test for functional vision problems. The behavioral optometrist may perform 20-30 inter-related tests to probe all the visual systems for visual functions, not merely sight! Functional vision testing requires at least 30 minutes of the doctor's testing time (not talking time). Otherwise, you may be sure the testing you requested was not adequately performed.

The behavioral evaluation may detect a functional vision problem of complexity sufficient to require a second visit. Many parents do not understand this because of their own experiences with quick sight-only examinations, so they do not make the appointment for a second examination. A functional vision exam record (containing 21 tests) was developed by the OEP Foundation and is used by many functional-behavioral vision specialists.

Give the optometrist you select to evaluate your child's vision a copy of the Performance-based Vision and Medical Observation Checklist you have prepared. You might also include a copy of the Educator's Guide (p. 46) completed by your child's teacher. The results of the Performance Vision Stress Test discussed on page 49 would also be useful. These will help your optometrist gain a realistic picture of your child's problems.

SCREEN YOUR OPTOMETRIST FORM

This copy of the **Screen Your Optometrist** form is to help you choose a doctor. If the practitioner does not test by these methods and measurements, problems will not be diagnosed and your child will continue to have functional vision problems. Copy and use the Screen Your Optometrist form that follows as many times as necessary to locate the vision specialist most qualified to test for and correct your child's vision problems.

1. Do you test for and correct accommodation (focusing) facility with +2 and -2 diopter flippers?

2. Do you test for and correct lateral vergence facility (lateral eye alignment and speed) using prism flippers with 3 diopters base in and 12 diopters base out?

3. Do you test for and correct vertical vergence ranges (vertical eye alignment) using single prisms base up and base down?

4. Do you test for and correct eye movement while the child is answering questions that make him/her think?

5. Will you tell me if my child has crossed eyes or other problems that need special vision training activities which I cannot safely provide myself (under your direction)? If so, will you provide the vision care needed or help me find the right care?

6. If you find my child has a functional vision problem, will you tell me how to correct it?

7. Will you order vision training equipment (if required) so that I can do training with my child at home? Under your supervision, as needed? Will you show me how to use it?

8 Will you send a written report to my child's teacher and other professionals?

Remember that you will have a fee to pay for this type of testing. Charges may vary but the costs cannot be compared to those for the basic type of test (for which the cost was around $30 in 1997). The standard "quick" exam only tests several aspects of the vision system as it relates to learning. Anyone with a learning problem needs the comprehensive testing discussed in this book.

Vision Skills Necessary For School Success

Over 80 percent of what your child learns in school is through the eyes. The vision activities listed below will teach your child how to move, focus and aim the eyes where she or he wants to look. Tell your child these activities will make school work easier and will help: improve sports performance, speed up copying from the chalkboard or a book and improve the level of understanding of what is read. When these activities can be done well, your child will probably begin reading for pleasure.

You, the parent, must make a commitment to do these vision training activities with your child 15 minutes (30 is better) a day 5 days a week (7 is better). **Children sent to their room or off by themselves to do these activities may not show any improvement.** The more time spent together, the faster the progress. If the parent does the activities with the child (parents do one activity while the child does another in some cases) the time required is usually cut in half. Doing the activities with the child motivates the youngster. If you work with your child every day but do not do the activities yourself, the time required to correct the problems will still be less than if the child works alone.

A chart has been provided for you and your child to keep a record of improvement. If there is any week in which your child does not make significant gains, ask your optometrist for suggestions. Once vision training activities are begun, do them quickly and efficiently, always looking for improvement in school and home. The child sees his progress and works even harder. A child who does the activities alone, without this encouragement, may do the activities incorrectly, waste time and become discouraged. If vision training time drags out over months or is dropped and continued a year or so later, the child will probably rebel and refuse to do the training.

By participating in your child's vision training activities, you may soon find you are reading more efficiently and for pleasure, enjoying night driving and not minding paperwork.

The following are the **minimum** vision training activities we believe necessary to teach the child to move, aim and focus his eyes efficiently. Our research shows these activities will help 70 percent of the affected students to be symptom-free and begin reading for pleasure in four weeks. In our experience about 30 percent of the students labeled learning disabled, visual dyslexic, attention deficit disordered and attention deficit hyperactive disordered have been moved out of special education after successfully completing these vision training activities. (These activities will not correct Down's Syndrome or cerebral palsy or other organic conditions. They can, however, help even these children work to their potential.) When these activities have been mastered, behavioral optometrists have many additional activities they can use if you wish your child's visual system to be fine tuned.

Equipment necessary to teach functional vision skills:

Equipment	**Problem**
+2/-2 flippers	Focusing
Prisms-diopters 1,2,3,4,6,8	Eye Alignment
Brock String	Focusing & Eye Alignment

Optional equipment to check suppression:

Red/green reading bar

Red/green glasses

See Resources page 42 in the back for places to purchase this equipment, which must be ordered by a vision specialist. (Note that schools starting a vision training program will need three sets of this equipment.) The next few pages outline the following skills and the activities to correct functional vision problems:

cognitive pursuit;

near point of convergence;

accommodation (focusing);

lateral & vertical eye alignment.

Skill: Cognitive Pursuit The ability to keep a clear image of a moving target while thinking is cognitive pursuit. This skill allows a child to look from word to word while reading and to comprehend the written material. The individual's oral reading flows smoothly and she is able to copy efficiently from the chalkboard or book.

A child who can not think while moving his eyes is often a slow, choppy reader with very poor comprehension. All of his energy goes into looking from word to word. If he moves his head while reading, he probably skips little two letter words and/or reverses three letter words (saw-was). He is using his neck muscles instead of his eye muscles. The neck muscles are not fine enough to control looking from word to word. A child with these difficulties may copy inaccurately and slowly.

Cognitive Pursuit Activities: One activity performed three minutes daily (choose one of two activities).

Goal: Child's eyes always on the target and seeing a clear image while thinking receives a score of good. A child who meets this goal to begin with does not need this activity. Most children will be done with this activity in two to four weeks.

Activity 1. Equipment: pencil with a small letter pasted on the eraser.

Move the pencil with a target letter on the eraser in a plane about 16 inches from the child's nose in all directions (figure 8s, diagonals, straight lines, etc.) at about twice the speed of the second hand on a clock. Be sure your child can keep the letter clear while following the target with his eyes. When the child can do this, ask him to count, say the alphabet, spell or answer math fact questions while following the target.

For example, a young child can count to ten or one hundred, add one plus one, say the alphabet, spell his name forward or backward. An older child can answer questions such as 7 x 8 = ____ or 6 x 9 + 5 = ____, name states and their capitals and spell difficult words.

In a school setting: Have three students watch the same target. Ask a question that requires thinking for an answer. Pause, then say the name of the child you wish to answer the question.

Activity 2. Equipment: ball with letters glued to it, suspended from ceiling on string.

Hang the ball from the ceiling low enough so that your child can just touch the ball with the tips of his fingers while lying on his back. As the ball swings, ask your child questions appropriate for his age while he watches the ball move parallel with his eyes and sees a letter on the ball clearly. (Later, for variety, this activity can be done from a standing position, with a shortened string.)

In a school setting: Have six students watch the same target. Ask a thinking question. Pause, then say the name of the child you wish to answer the question.

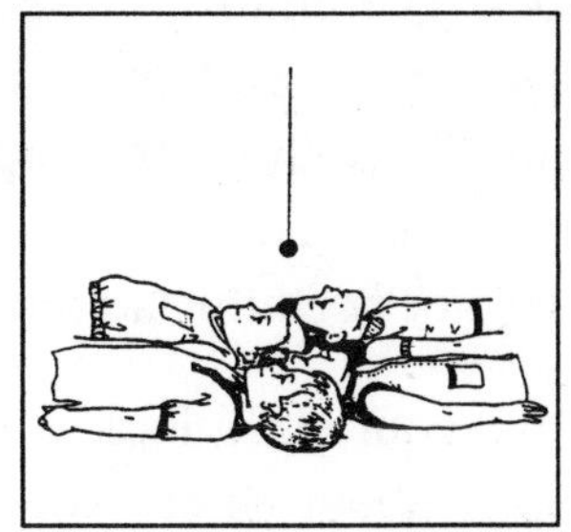

Chart your child's progress weekly. A **Weekly Progress Chart** has been provided on p. 17 as well as in the Appendix. **Use <u>good,</u> <u>fair</u> or <u>poor</u> depending on the difficulty the child shows following the target letter.** If there is great difficulty, mark poor. If the child is often off target, write fair. If your child is always on target and sees the letter clearly, write good. Significant gains should be seen weekly in eye movement if the activities are done five minutes a day, five days a week. If you do not see weekly progress, consult your optometrist.

Skill: Near Point Of Convergence (NPC) The ability to see and hold clear a single image while following a target from 3 feet in to 2 inches using the two eyes together is near point of convergence.

A child with good near point of convergence can read a book for long periods of time without developing headaches or double vision. The attention span for near work is good and avoidance behaviors are not shown. The child who has poor near point of convergence (trouble following a pencil eraser in to two inches from his nose and following it back out) often has a short attention span, day dreams and may develop headaches, see double and/or avoid reading.

Near Point Of Convergence Activities: One activity performed five minutes daily. As soon as the child is good at Activity 1, begin Activity 2. As soon as the child is good at Activity 2, begin Activity 3.

Activity 1. Equipment: pencil with an eraser.

Goal: The child follows the target with both eyes together to within 2 inches of the nose, then smoothly follows the target back out four times in succession. Any child who already has this skill does not need this activity.

Have your child look at the eraser on the end of a pencil about three feet from his nose. Tell your child to keep watching the eraser as you move the pencil towards him and back out. Move the pencil slowly toward his nose and back out, four times without stopping. He should be able to follow the target with his eyes to within two inches of his nose and back out four times.

One eye may "kick out," which means the child will see two pencils. If you have a hard time seeing whether your child's eyes are following the target, move the pencil side to side slightly as you move it towards and away from his nose.

In a school setting: Group students in pairs. Students take turns moving the target for the other one to watch while the volunteer supervises.

Chart your child's progress weekly by recording how close to the nose the child can see the target (pencil) as single when following the target in and back out.

Weekly progress can be expected. If you do not see weekly progress, consult your optometrist.

Activity 2. To be done as soon as the child can do Activity 1 proficiently.

Equipment: the Brock String. A string 10 feet long with 3 beads on it (will use 10 foot strings in Activity 3). Each bead has letters on it.

Goal: The child is able to see the letter on the near bead clearly and see the string correctly and quickly when the near bead is two inches from his nose and see the letter clearly on the far bead when it is at 3 feet. A child already possessing this skill need not do this activity.

Have your child hold one end of the string to the tip of his nose. Place the beads 1 foot and 3 feet from his nose. Have the child look at the bead three feet away and focus on a letter on the bead and ask the child what he sees. The child should see two strings and two close beads. The strings should appear to come together at the far bead and make a V.

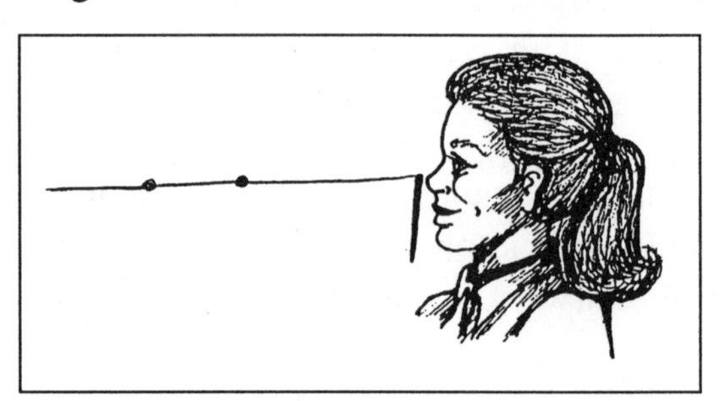

If the child does not see two strings, alternately cover and uncover one eye quickly with your hand until two strings are seen. If this does not work, cover and uncover the other eye until two strings are seen. Jiggling the string is another way to help the child see two strings. It may be necessary to move the bead out farther or in as close as 6 inches. If the child does not see two strings, he is suppressing the vision in one eye. This may happen after eye muscle (strabismus) surgery. If your child can not see both strings after many attempts to see two, stop the activity and consult your optometrist.

Continue having the child look at one bead and then the other bead. He should always see two strings and one bead where he is looking while at the same time being aware of two of the other beads. The letter on the bead at which he is looking should be clear. (By getting the letter clear and at the same time aligning the eyes, you are working on both focusing and eye alignment.)

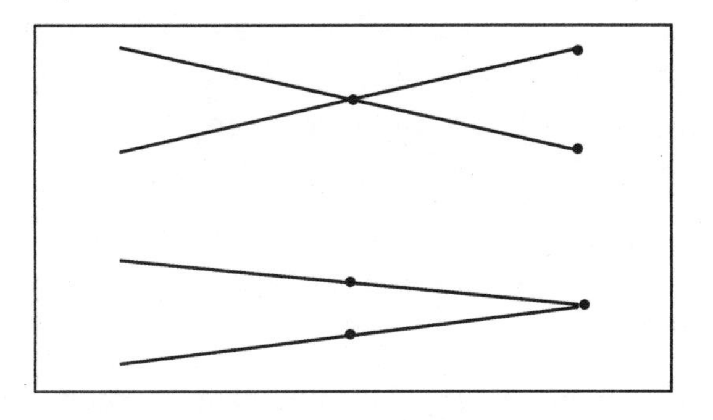

If the child looks at the near bead, the strings should cross there and make an X. When looking at the far bead, the strings will form a long V with two beads closer. The letters on the bead should be clear when looking at that bead. When this can be done easily, ask the child to make sure the X (the crossing of the strings) is precisely within the bead.

In a school setting: Have three students do this activity at the same time. Each student holds the end of the Brock String on the tip of his nose. The volunteer holds the other end of the three strings. The volunteer says, "Look at the close bead—far bead—close bead—far bead—," and so on. Watch the eyes aim in and out. Keep moving the close bead nearer to the nose.

Chart your child's progress. **Record how close to the nose the child has moved the near bead while being able to see it and the string correctly.** Weekly progress can be expected. Any week you do not see progress, consult your optometrist.

Activity 3. To be done as soon as the child can do Activity 2 well.

Equipment: the Brock String: A string at least 10 feet long with 3 beads on it, with letters on each of the beads.

Goal: the same as Activity 2, except that the far bead is 10 feet away from the nose. If your child can see the beads and strings correctly, this activity is not needed.

Have your child hold one end of the string to the tip of his nose. Place the beads 2 inches, 3 feet, and 10 feet from his nose. Have the child look at the bead 3 feet away and focus on a letter on the bead. Ask the child what he sees. The correct answer is two strings and two close beads and two far beads. The strings should appear to cross at the middle bead and make an X. Have your child look at the near bead. Ask him what he sees. The correct answer is two strings meeting in an X at the near bead. He should see one near bead, two middle beads and two far beads. The strings look continuous and do not have any gaps in them.

Have your child look at the far bead. Ask him what he sees. The correct answer is two strings meeting in a V at the far bead. He should see one far bead, two middle beads and two near beads. The strings look continuous and do not have any gaps in them. Continue having the child look from bead to bead. Move the middle bead to different distances. Your child should always see two solid strings without any gaps in them. The strings should appear to cross in the middle of the bead at which the child is looking. He should see one bead where he is looking while at the same time being aware of two of each of the other beads. The letter on the bead at which he is looking should be clear. (By getting the letter clear, and at the same time aligning the eyes, you are working on both focusing and eye alignment.)

In a school setting: Have three students do this activity at the same time. Each student holds the end of the Brock String on the tip of his or her nose. The volunteer holds the other end of the three strings and says, "Look at the close bead—far bead—close bead—far bead—," and so on. Watch the eyes aim in and out. Keep moving the close bead nearer to the nose.

Chart your child's progress weekly. **Record how far from the nose the child has moved the far bead while being able to see beads and the string correctly.** Weekly progress can be expected.

Skill: Accommodation (Focusing) Accommodation is focusing. Focusing the eyes is similar to focusing binoculars. The lens in the eye must be round to see something close and flat to see an object far away. Normally, we are born with 16 diopters of focusing ability. We lose one quarter of a diopter every year after that. For most of us, by the time we are around forty years old, we need bifocals for reading. Parents who have lost their focusing ability can not do this activity with their child.

A child with good focusing ability can look at all different distances quickly and efficiently and see clearly at each distance. This child can copy quickly from the chalkboard, overhead projector screen, a math book or English book. Students with good focusing skills can use a work sheet with a computer screen or look at the teacher during lectures then look down at their papers quickly to write notes.

Accommodation (Focusing) Activities: One activity performed five minutes daily.

Goal: The child reads a book from a distance of 16 inches and uses both sides of the flippers. If a child is good at this activity at the beginning, the activity need not be continued.

Equipment: +2/-2 diopter flippers, a book and a reading stand. The reading stand may be made by bending a metal bookend over to about 80 degrees. You can find bookends at places like KMart or Walmart.

Move the book stand close enough to your child for the print to be clear when both sides of the flippers are used. Have your child read a sentence, flip the lenses over and read another sentence from the book. **Record the distance from the eye to the book weekly.** Keep reading and flipping and moving the book back until the child can read using both sides of the flippers from a distance of 16 inches.

In a school setting: The volunteer watches three students; they each have their own flippers, reading stand and book.

Chart your child's progress weekly. Most children can move the book 2 or 3 inches farther away each week. The length of time required to complete this activity depends on the severity of the problem and the time spent on this activity. Your child may reach the goal of 14-16 inches in two to three weeks, working five minutes a day, five days a week.

Significant gains can be expected each week; if this is not the case, consult your optometrist.

Skill: Eye Alignment The ability to aim the eyes in and out (lateral), up or down (vertical) is eye alignment. This skill makes it possible for a child to aim his eyes at a word at different distances and see a single image of each letter. As a child looks at the chalkboard, the eyes aim nearly parallel and immediately see the clear image of each letter. At any distance, the image is immediately clear and single and stays clear and single.

Poor lateral eye alignment causes headaches and/or short attention span. Poor vertical alignment causes a child to skip lines when reading. This is often detectable when a child uses a finger or a marker to keep his place, tilts his head while reading, gets too close to his work, and/or covers one eye. Many times, the child with a vertical problem has a hard time learning the alphabet and does not learn to read. This problem may also cause avoidance

Weekly Progress Chart

Name: ______________________________

Activity	Week 1	Week 2	Week 3	Week 4	Week 5	Week 6

Name: ______________________________

Activity	Week 1	Week 2	Week 3	Week 4	Week 5	Week 6

behavior, sometimes to the extent that the child is labeled Attention Deficit Disorder (ADD) or Attention Deficit Hyperactive Disorder (ADHD), learning disabled or visual dyslexic. Other indicators of lateral alignment problems occur when letters appear to swim, to move and/or to look double.

Lateral Eye Alignment Activity: One activity performed 5 minutes daily.

Goal: The child can see the target as a single image from 4 feet with the 8 diopter prism holding the stick down and flipping the prism back and forth so that the thick part is first towards the nose and then away from it (base in and base out). If a child is good at this, the activity is not needed.

> Equipment: 4, 6 and 8 diopter prisms on sticks. A ¼ inch vertical line 2 inches long made with a marker and placed on the wall or refrigerator at the child's eye level, for a target.
>
> (The number 4, 6 or 8 is printed on the thick side of the prism.)

To correct lateral eye alignment problems, start with a 4 diopter prism on a stick. Have your child look at the target at eye level while standing 12 inches from it. Have the child hold the prism by the stick straight down from one eye. A single image should be seen. Have her flip the lens over; only one line should be seen. If two are seen, have the child look at it until she can make it into one. If it is difficult to see it as one, having the child lean forwards and backwards may help. Blinking may help also.

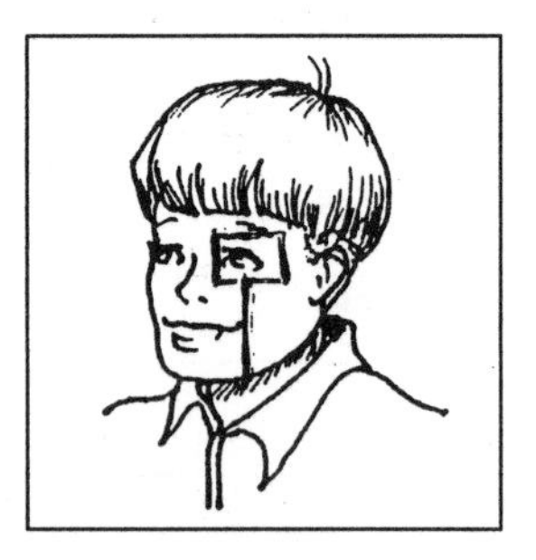

When a single image is seen each time the prism is flipped, have the child move back 3 inches and do the process again; have him keep moving back 3 inches until this can be done from 4 feet. Then have the child stand 12 inches from the target and use the 6 diopter prism. Continue with the 8 diopter prism. Move from 12 inches out to 4 feet with each prism.

In a school setting: The volunteer watches three students, each with the appropriate prism. The students all watch the same target.

Your child should be able to progress from 4 diopter to 8 diopter prisms in 4 weeks working 5 minutes a day on this activity. **Each week record which prism the student is using and the distance from the target.** Significant gains can be expected each week; if not, consult your optometrist.

Vertical Eye Alignment Activity: One activity performed five minutes daily

Goal: The child can see the target as a single image from 4 feet using the 4 diopter prism holding the stick horizontally and flipping the prism back and forth so that the thick part is first up and then down (base up and base down). If your child can already do this, this activity is not needed.

> Equipment: 1, 2, 3 and 4 diopter prisms on sticks. (The number 1, 2, 3 or 4 is printed on the thick side of the prism.) A target made of a ¼ inch horizontal line 2 inches long on the refrigerator or wall at the child's eye level.

To correct vertical eye alignment problems, start with a 1 diopter prism. Have your child hold the stick horizontally, to the left or right from the eye and look at a target at eye level through the prism while standing 12 inches from the target. One line should be seen. Flip the lens over; one line should be seen. If two are seen, have the child look at it and make it into one. If this is difficult, suggest the child lean his body forwards and backwards, which may help. After one line is seen each time the prism is flipped, the child moves back 3 inches, and the process is repeated. When this can be done from 4 feet, return to 12 inches and use the 2 diopter prism. Continue with 2, 3 and 4 diopter prisms. With each prism move out to 4 feet.

In a school setting: The volunteer watches three students, each with the appropriate prism. The students all watch the same target. You should see significant progress each week. If not, consult your optometrist.

Medical Problems

Allergies are a second cause of behavior and learning problems and may be more common than vision problems. The American Allergy Association says, "Allergies don't cause everything, but they can cause anything."[25] Allergies can cause all types of emotional, educational, behavioral and medical problems. Educational symptoms may include hyperactivity, poor handwriting, clumsiness, loudness, irritability, inability to get along with others, inability to recall facts or how to spell words, letter reversals (b as d, etc.), **failure to turn in assignments on time**, inability to sit still as well as good days and bad days. These symptoms may be mild to severe and are not widely recognized as allergy-related by the traditional allergist.[26, 27, 28, 29] Many traditional allergists believe that allergies can only affect limited, specific areas of the body: nose, eyes, lungs, skin and intestines. The usual tests and screening by traditional allergists do not pick up the types of problems which may be causing learning, behavior or emotional difficulties for your child.[30]

Many foods, chemicals, molds, pollens and air pollutants at home and at school can cause allergies.[31] Substances called chemical mediators are released during allergic reactions and travel all over the body, not just to "accepted" areas such as the lungs or nose.[32] Yeast infections that can occur after a child has taken antibiotics can leave the child handicapped in ways that show themselves as: short attention span, hyperactive, loud, poor speller, behavior problems, inability to get along with others and/or irritable.[33] Monosodium glutamate (MSG), a food additive, and NutraSweet, a sweetener in many foods, especially diet drinks, may cause the same reactions in some individuals.[34, 35] Many children who are suffering from non-conventional allergic reactions are being incorrectly labeled as having learning disabilities, auditory dyslexia, attention deficit disorder, attention deficit hyperactive disorder and other problems. Specialists in environmental medicine believe it is possible that any area of the body can be affected by an allergy to a food or to a chemical sensitivity.

Be an informed parent. Before going to your physician, read literature by prominent doctors in the field of allergy-related behavioral, emotional and educational problems. Titles in the Reading List at the back of this book may be at your local library. If not, ask your librarian to check if the book you require is available from another library for you (interlibrary loan). Also, complete the Performance-based Vision and Medical Observation checklist for your child (see p. 5). This will give your doctor a realistic picture of your child's academic and social problems and help both of you as you discuss how to approach your child's problems. The child's teacher may be able to help you with this record.

Parents have a choice about how to treat a medical problem. For information on causes and treatment options read: elimination diet (p. 20), antihistamines (p. 21), extract therapy (p. 20), other medical problems (p. 22), nutrition (p. 22), yeast (p. 22), biofeedback (p. 23), NutraSweet and MSG (p. 22).

Elimination Diet If you think a food allergy is part of your child's difficulties, you may wish to try an elimination diet, which is designed to pinpoint what foods are causing an allergic reaction. Make a list of your child's and your favorite foods and beverages. People often crave the foods to which they are allergic. If the list includes dairy products, wheat or flour, corn, sugar, chocolate, caffeine, citrus, eggs or yeast, you have prime suspects.

At least two kinds of elimination diets are available: a single food elimination diet and a multifood elimination diet.[36] When using the single food elimination diet, one food is eliminated from the diet for four days to a week while a diary of any reactions or improvements is kept. When the symptoms are gone, this food is then added to the diet to see the reaction. You keep trying foods until symptoms are eliminated. When using a multifood elimination diet, many foods are eliminated at the same time then added back one food at a time. Reactions to each food are recorded. If the elimination diet did not work, the person looks closely to see if the suspected food was eaten in some other food (milk or wheat flour in gravy, sugar in bread or cereal).

In *The Impossible Child* (Doris Rapp, M.D.) and *Help for the Hyperactive Child* (which has six pages of endorsements by medical and learning specialists) and *Your Hard-to-Raise Child* (both by William G. Crook, M.D.), the authors describe elimination diets and list allowed and forbidden foods. Dr. Crook gives good menus that show it is possible to eat well and still eliminate some foods. Before Dr. Crook sees a patient, he has parents try his elimination diet with their child. Many parents solve the major part of their child's problems before they reach the doctor's office.[37] Dr. Crook reports solving three out of four children's hyperactive problems by eliminating the foods causing the allergy. Dr. Rapp's book *Is This Your Child?* has a helpful section, "Diets That Help Quickly." Dr. Rapp's non-profit organization, Practical Allergy Research Foundation, P.O. Box 60, Buffalo, NY 14223, 716-875-5578, will send you free, an excellent, 4-page multifood elimination diet.

It is not simple to eliminate wheat, milk, citrus or corn. To leave out wheat, you must eliminate bread, cereals and wheat pastas, gravies, white or wheat flour, cake, pastry, cookies, thickened commercial soups and vitamin E. Remember that milk includes dairy products with milk, anything made with milk (cakes or pancakes), sour cream, ice cream and butter. Eliminating citrus means leaving out oranges, grapefruit, lemons, tangerines and limes. The long list of foods with corn can be found in the books mentioned above. When you go to your doctor, take the book *Help for the Hyperactive Child* and the Performance-based Observation Checklist you and the teacher have completed.

Extract Therapy Doctors of environmental medicine use standards and tests for allergies different from those of traditional allergists.[38, 39] Drs. Doris Rapp and William Crook are doctors of environmental medicine.

Provocation-Neutralization allergy treatment is one technique doctors of environmental medicine often use. A solution of the substance to which the child is allergic is given as an injection or is placed under the tongue. In *Is This Your Child?*, Dr. Rapp describes (p. 488) one of environmental medicine's techniques. First, Dr. Rapp has the child write his name. She then injects the child with a substance identified as a probable cause of his problems. Every few minutes, she asks the child to write his name. If the handwriting deteriorates, she gives the child an antidote of the substance. If the handwriting immediately improves, the problem's cause and the treatment have been identified. Dr. Doris Rapp uses handwriting as a diagnostic tool for allergies.[40] To locate an informed doctor specializing in environmental medicine see p. 42 in the Resource section. Remember, you must be satisfied with the doctor. If you are not, try another one.

Antihistamines A range of antihistamines can often be used to treat allergies that cause problems which lead to false labels for a child: auditory dyslexic, attention deficit disordered, attention deficit hyperactive disordered, emotionally disturbed and learning disabled. (In the books *Smart But Feeling Dumb* and *Total Concentration*, H. N. Levinson, M.D., cites many case studies in which parents reported children doing much better in school while taking antihistamines for colds. **Most students the authors referred to medical doctors and who were given antihistamines improved dramatically, both academically and in behavior, within two weeks.** <u>Students who did not turn in assignments</u> **were referred to their family doctor, who would prescribe a trial 2-week course of antihistamines.** Over half of the time there were positive results. It appears most of the information a student has been exposed to is stored in the brain, but allergies block the retrieval of this information. When a child starts taking an antihistamine, and the dosage has been properly adjusted, she or he can recall and use all the information stored in the brain quickly without great effort. An allergy can settle in any part of the brain and cause all kinds of learning, behavioral and emotional problems.[41]

Dr. Del Stigler, a Fellow of the American Academy of Environmental Medicine, suggests the reason antihistamines work in this manner has to do with their chemical composition. Some antihistamines have chemical compositions similar to that of the neurotransmitters which form the chemical links between nerve cells in the brain and may simply be enhancing these neurotransmitters.

Have your medical doctor review your child's history of academic and social problems, including the Performance-based Vision and Medical Checklist which you filled out. If your doctor and you believe it is a possibility that an allergy problem may be causing your child's educational and/or behavioral problems, **ask your doctor to treat your child with antihistamines for a two-week trial period.**

If the antihistamine works, you may begin to see a positive behavior change within three days. Watch for one or more of these educational signs of change: better grades, improved handwriting, writing without reversals, better spelling, knowledge of math facts, turning in assignments, acceptable behavior, getting along better with classmates and siblings, improved concentration and not as loud or irritable. Or, you no longer wish to give the child away.

Your doctor will have your child's medical history and will know if there is a medical reason for not prescribing antihistamines (such as an allergy to antihistamines or a possible reaction with other medications your child is taking). If you and your doctor are reluctant to try antihistamines, you may wish to try an elimination diet or you may wish to take your child directly to an environmental allergist for testing.

If the antihistamine works but makes the child sleepy, Dr. Levinson cuts the dosage in half or in quarters.[42] If one type of antihistamine does not work, ask your doctor to try another; there are six major chemical groups of antihistamines. Some children need to take antihistamines all the time with the possible exception of weekends and summers (non-school time). Others are able to take the antihistamines effectively only when symptoms recur. Be sure to communicate any changes in dosage and the results with your child's doctor.

You and your doctor may decide to continue antihistamines indefinitely, especially if your child has to take them only occasionally. Or you may try identifying what is causing the allergy. There are many possible causes: air, molds, chemicals, perfumes or foods. The problem with giving antihistamines as needed is that parents sometimes fail to recognize when their child has slipped back into the old allergic pattern until there is real trouble again. In our experience, this happens about a third of the time. One advantage of an elimination diet over antihistamines is consistency.

If your child's problem is very severe, a doctor in environmental medicine can help you identify what is causing the allergy and correct it. See Resources at the back of this book for the address of the American Academy of Environmental Medicine.

Nutrition Every person is biochemically unique. Though our needs differ, we all must have vitamins, minerals, trace elements and essential fatty acids. With the food additives and junk food eaten today, supplemental vitamins are often necessary. As Dr. Flach wrote in the book *Rickie,* his daughter Rickie, institutionalized for over ten years as a schizophrenic, was able to live a normal life once her nutrition, mineral imbalance and vision problems had been corrected. The body needs thousands of different chemicals, which it makes from about fifty raw materials. If children do not eat enough of the right foods to provide these raw materials, including numerous amino acids, fatty acids, minerals, vitamins, water, glucose and fiber, they will be unable to reach their full potential.

Other Medical Problems High levels of yeast in the body create possible medical problems. If behavioral or learning difficulties or repeated ear infections occur after your child has taken an antibiotic (amoxicillin, septra, ceclor, augmentin), advise your doctor and determine the proper treatment. A yeast-free, sugar-free diet and Nystatin program may be the answer. (Nystatin is an antifungal medication that controls the growth of yeast and yeast-like fungi.)[43] All of Dr. Crook's books have indepth descriptions of behavior and treatments for yeast infection.

Inner-ear problems are reported by Dr. Levinson in his books *Smart But Feeling Dumb* and *Total Concentration* as causes of dyslexia, learning disabilities and attention deficit disorder. He uses an anti-motion medication and antihistamines to correct the problems. It appears that the symptoms Dr. Levinson treats with medication, Drs. Rapp and Crook correct with diet and/or extract therapy.

Excitotoxins such as NutraSweet (aspartame) and MSG (monosodium glutamate) can cause brain damage[44] and are suspected of having a link to Alzheimer's, Parkinson's and other nervous system diseases. MSG may cause headaches, gastrointestinal symptoms, facial flush, depression, seizures, incontinence, hyperactivity, irritability, whining, yelling, unreasonableness, violent behavior and other symptoms.[45] It is thought that MSG can cause a person to be obese or short and can cause difficulty in reproduction.[46] MSG can also cause asthma symptoms. Symptoms can be mild or severe. To those who can not metabolize it effectively, MSG works like a poison. Intolerance to MSG is not an allergic reaction but a "true drug effect."[47]

MSG is the most frequently used food additive, after salt and pepper. It is used in nearly any kind of food you may buy. Even the biggest, most respected companies use it. **Careful reading of labels is a must.** This sounds easy, but the presence of MSG is often disguised by such descriptions as: hydrolyzed protein, hydrolyzed vegetable protein, hydrolyzed plant protein, protein hydrolysate, hydrolyzed oat flour, plant protein extract, textured protein, all natural flavorings, vegetable powder, sodium caseinate, calcium caseinate, autolyzed yeast, yeast extract, gelatin and flavor enhancers.[48]

Where will you find MSG? In many items.[49] Fast-food restaurants often serve foods containing MSG.[50]

NutraSweet contains aspertame and is used in most diet drinks. NutraSweet actually causes brain cells to die. It is particularly bad for the very young and elderly. If you read *Excitotoxins: The Taste That Kills* by Russell L. Blaylock, M.D., you may never drink another diet drink again and will carefully look at food labels. To locate an environmental doctor in your area, see Resource (p. 42). Remember, you must be satisfied with the doctor. If you are not, try another.

EEG Biofeedback A very successful procedure, EEG biofeedback has been used to correct hyperactivity and some learning problems. An electrode is connected to the head of the child or the adult who is being helped. The child then controls a computer game through concentration—the Pac Man game is used for one activity—the stronger the concentration, the brighter the figures on the screen and the more quickly they move through the mazes. The charter school in Minneapolis, A chance to Grow, uses three of these machines. A number of programs are used to correct different problems; seizures, bed-wetting, learning and attention problems. At the school, all children who are being given Ritalin are placed on biofeedback. Within a short time, these children no longer need Ritalin. The school reports that children with learning and attention problems benefit from biofeedback treatment through improved impulse control, ability to plan, ability to concentrate, short term memory, above average gains in reading skills and in generally feeling better about themselves.

If All Else Fails

If you have tried vision training activities and your child can focus, aim and move her/his eyes and there are still problems...

If you have taken your child to a doctor listed by the American Academy of Environmental Medicine who has evaluated your child for allergies, yeast infection, MSG and nutrition and there are still problems...

If you have tried antihistamines and there are still problems...

If you have tried EEG biofeedback and there are still problems...

If you have used a guided reader program (p. 31) to speed the child's reading and the template program (p. 30) and there are still problems...

If you have tried all these techniques and nothing has worked, perhaps Ritalin or one of the newer medications for distractibility and impulsivity should be tried. Experts agree that medication of this type should only be used as a last resort and only as a part of a total treatment program that includes psychological, educational and social measures.

Be informed. Request information from the physician who prescribes the drug; learn about the many possible side effects as well as the expected benefits. Parents, teachers and physicians must work closely to monitor the results of such medication.

Children – Examples

■ Eric

As a third grader, Eric could not read his birthday cards even though he had an I.Q. of 150+. He had already been retained once, as a first grader. The school thought he had a self-esteem problem and wanted to know what his parents were doing wrong at home. They also suggested that Eric have a home computer on which to do his writing. Eric's parents asked Allan Crane if he worked with dyslexics. He said he did and asked them whether Eric was an auditory or a visual dyslexic. The school had not told them.

At the author's suggestion, Eric's parents took him to an optometrist and to their family doctor. It was determined that Eric had both visual (eye movement, eye alignment and focusing) and medical problems. Eric did vision training activities and began taking an antihistamine.

Eric's handwriting and spelling improved dramatically in two weeks with use of the antihistamine; he took half a tablet each morning and night, excluding weekends and vacations. Eric reported that he did not have to think how to spell words, he knew. He said, "The cloud clears earlier in the day." His classmates could tell by his handwriting if Eric had forgotten to take his antihistamine. Eric also could tell and soon became very responsible about taking it. Eric's brother and sister reported that he was easier to live with when he was on the antihistamine.

After just six weeks of vision training activities, Eric began to read for pleasure (he used a flashlight under the covers to read at night) and was making As and Bs in the regular classroom. In the fourth grade, Eric was placed in gifted classes. As a high school student, Eric still reads for pleasure and continues to make good grades in honors classes. Two years ago Eric stopped taking antihistamines. He also started competitive swimming at that time.

It is interesting to note that Eric's brother and sister were in gifted classes at the time Eric was having trouble in school. Eric's brother had been tested for allergies and was receiving allergy treatments. Eric had never displayed any obvious allergy symptoms such as rashes, dark circles under the eyes, dry skin or lips, runny nose and no one had suspected Eric of having allergies. The doctor first put Eric on Dimetapp with initial but short-lived improvement. Next he prescribed Tavis-D which did not lose its effectiveness and to which Eric did not develop an immunity.

■ William

Allen met William when working with special education children in William's school and using the Performance-based Vision Stress (PVS) Test. William was a sixth grader and had been placed in special education classes and labeled learning disabled. He was irritable, a poor reader and hated school and the world. William had done eye training activities under the direction of an optometrist as a four-year-old because his eyes did not track properly. His parents did not start William in kindergarten until he was six because he obviously did not have the necessary skills. William had completed the first five grades with fair marks and without negative teacher comments. Then he hit middle school with its multiple schedule of teachers and increased demands, including smaller print.

William failed the PVS Test. He failed the near-far copying and reported symptoms after the test. He was referred to an optometrist for visual problems and to the family doctor for medical problems. Vision training activities were done to correct focusing and eye alignment problems and antihistamines (Dimetapp) taken. William's mother reported, "It was like night and day, the difference. He was no longer moody. He could remember things; before, he would forget. His handwriting was a lot better. He could do better on tests, but on days he forgot his Dimetapp, he was back to the same ways." William still had trouble reading as fast as other children in his class. William then read on a guided reader and increased his reading speed to 175 words per minute with good comprehension. William's handwriting and spelling improved when he took his Dimetapp.

Later, William's mother reported, "William is now a 10th grader, a very well rounded teenager with confidence and determination to do well. He made the honor roll for three quarters and is ready to start plans for college." On William's report cards, he received such comments as the following (February 15, 1996): "I really like having William in my class. He sets a great example for other students by being involved and trying so hard. Thanks."

William is allergic to wheat, dust and mold, which cannot be avoided on his father's farm. As William helps more on the farm, his allergies increase and school becomes more difficult. Although William never forgets anything, oral tests are frequently necessary because his writing is often unreadable. At this point, the authors are recommending William go to a doctor of environmental medicine for extract therapy and an elimination diet.

■ Claudia

In February, the first-grade teacher told Claudia's mother that Claudia should repeat the grade. Claudia reversed the letters b-d, n-u, h-y. She did not recognize all the letters, had a poor sight vocabulary and had tested poorly on a visual perception test given at school.

Allen met Claudia when she was taken to an optometrist. Claudia was diagnosed as having poor functional vision skills and was referred to the family doctor for allergies. She did templates and vision training activities. The family physician prescribed the antihistamine liquid Dimetapp for a two-week trial period. It helped. She took it on an as-needed basis. In June of that year, Claudia received the top reader award in her class. Claudia is now in high school, still making good grades and reading for pleasure.

■ Shirley

Claudia's sister Shirley, a tenth grader, had been in special education since kindergarten. The author worked with her when she came to the optometrist's office. She was given template exercises and vision training activities and was referred to her family doctor for allergies. The doctor put her on an antihistamine. Six weeks later, the school moved Shirley out of special education. Her special education teacher said he had never seen such progress. Shirley made A's, B's and C's in regular classes for the rest of her high school years. She wrote the following paper for tenth grade English.

A Life's Struggle

Do you know a person who is in a special class known as resource? I know one, that person was me. I can remember when I was in the first grade, I was put into the resource room. Usually around the same time every day I would put away my schoolwork and walk out of class to go to the resource room. When I returned I usually disrupted the class because my fellow classmates asked me where I had been? When I told them I was in the resource room, their reply was, "Isn't that where the dumb people go?" I would turn around and sink down into my chair, wishing I could disappear. I tried so hard to get out of the resource room that I spent many hours doing homework trying to get ahead. I even spent many summers in summer school, we even tried a tutor but nothing seemed to work. My parents who were supportive started to give up on me, but I felt that I had to keep on going.

But as time went on and things did not get any better I started to give up, too. I thought, what's the use, I'm no good. This was around the time my sister Claudia started seeing an eye therapist. She would come home doing all kinds of weird exercises with her eyes. Then my mom suggested for me to go see Allen Crane, too. I thought she was crazy, but to please her I went along with them to Claudia's next appointment.

When I arrived at the office I still thought this is crazy, just one big joke. But I went along with it, and I am glad I did, because in a few weeks my grades started to go up. And in the tenth grade, for the first time ever I got straight Bs with an exception of a C+ but I'm working on that one. This year is the first year I have been out of resource, it is a real chance to show everyone that I can do it on my own. But the battle is not over yet, I still must keep working on my skills and try to pick up on the subjects that I missed out on in my regular class like science, health, and history, which are my hardest subjects in school right now. Now that I have realized I can have almost any career I wish for but I must struggle with the ten year learning disability on my school record, and with that record I will have to struggle once more to fulfill another dream and that is to go to college. But please don't let kids suffer like I have, don't let them struggle throughout their

whole life, like I must do. Show them there are other possibilities. And never give up hope for them because they just might give up on themselves or they just might prove you wrong. Show them the light because they hold the future of our country.

■ Thomas

The first time Allan Crane worked with Thomas, then a fourth grader, Thomas did not know his math facts consistently. One day he would know them, the next day he would not. As his special education resource teacher, the author drilled him on his math facts and played math games all year. Thomas moved away but returned three years later.

The author was ready for Thomas with all kinds of computer math games that were supposed to teach math facts. Allan was actually disappointed when Thomas demonstrated that he knew his math facts. He gave twelve answers in eleven seconds from flash cards laid randomly on the table in front of him. He knew them all. You can imagine the author's surprise when two months later Thomas did not even know the answer to 3 x 6.

The author showed the boy's parents Dr. Levinson's book *Smart But Feeling Dumb*. After reading the book, they took Thomas to their family doctor who prescribed a continuing rotation with three days of Sudafed, three days of Tavis D and three days of Dimetapp. This rotation was used so that Thomas would not build up a tolerance for any of the three medications. Within 18 hours, Thomas was able to recall all his math facts. Incidentally, he also quit reversing b and d while he was taking antihistamines. Thomas continued to take antihistamines on an as-needed basis.

■ Christopher

When he was 18 months old, Christopher had trouble with asthma. Between the ages of 18 months and 5 years, he had to be rushed to the emergency room two or three times a month. He went through three inhalers a week for his asthma. Christopher was very pale, had shiners under his eyes, a runny nose and ear infections. He itched terribly, which caused many bizarre and embarrassing situations. He often covered his ears at loud sounds. Christopher was extremely noisy, often "spaced out," had severe mood swings and hourly temper tantrums. However, it was obvious Christopher was a very intelligent boy. As a five-year-old, he could spell many five-letter words.

Allan Crane saw Christopher when the boy was five years old. He was going right from one temper tantrum to another. His parents could not even take him to a restaurant to eat. They were completely at their wit's end. At the author's suggestion, Christopher was taken to an environmental doctor, who put Christopher on a diet and Nystatin to stop the yeast infection. Christopher was on Nystatin for about a year. The diet eliminated yeast, dairy products, sugar, food coloring, caramel flavoring and anything fermented. Overnight, Christopher was better. In two weeks he was a different child. As an 8-year-old Christopher is able to carry on a conversation, is a pleasure to have around, a straight A student and no longer has asthma symptoms. Life is much easier for the family.

Part II
The Parent–Teacher Team

You are a teacher hoping to help the parents of one or two of your students through the maze of uncertainties to unlock their child's potential. What can you and the parents do?

As a classroom teacher, you see students several hours a day involved in numerous activities. You know which students cause you concern. Schools do not allow you to refer to a specific doctor. How frustrating when unhappy parents return saying their child sees 20/20, there is nothing wrong with the child's eyes, or their medical doctor says there is nothing wrong with the child. The parents' section of this book will help parents find a doctor or doctors who will test their child for school-related problems. The videos by Doris Rapp, M.D. (on allergies) and P.A.V.E. (on vision) are also useful in helping parents realize the importance of choosing the right doctor to obtain the proper care (see Resources (p. 42) for addresses).

After reading this book, suggest that the parents read it also. After the parents have read the book, talk about the observations of the parents at home and the observations you make at school. Together, you and the parents will help the child reach her or his full potential.

Teacher Observations to Help Parents

Have the whole class copy something from the chalkboard such as their spelling or vocabulary words. Direct your students to lay their papers on your desk when they have completed the task. Allow them to choose something they want to do when they finish. For example, young students may go out to recess and older students may study for another class. The papers will be in a pile on your desk in order from the children who copied most quickly to those who copied most slowly. The last papers to come in are from students who experience visual difficulty when looking back and forth at those distances efficiently.

You will know vision problems are indicated when you observe a student get too near (closer than eight inches) to the book when reading, tilt his or her head, cover one eye, use a finger or a marker to keep the place while reading. A vision problem is also indicated when a student reads very slowly and choppily and/or does not comprehend what is read.

Have the students write from dictation a list of words they have not studied. Use a word list at about grade level (the Slosson Oral Reading Test or the Crane Word List in the back of the book). When you look at the papers, note if the student in question left obvious sounds out of words. An example is leaving out the d in under. Did the student leave out obvious sounds in three of the twenty words spelled? If so, this indicates a medical problem rather than a vision problem. Were any letters reversed (b-d, h-y, n-u, p-b)? Does the student have noticeably poor handwriting? These two problems are indicative of a medical problem. It is an advantage to have a teacher looking for these things, because the teacher has a basis of comparison while parents do not necessarily have that advantage. If you want this type of information on everyone in your class, you can give the Crane Word List (p. 48) to the whole class at one time (see the Reference section for directions).

As a teacher, you know if the student is not turning in assignments, is louder than other children, is clumsy, daydreams or is inattentive. These problems also indicate a medical problem.

Short attention span/hyperactivity can be either a medical or a vision problem

When you compare the results of your observations with those of the parents, you will be a lot closer to making correct referrals for the child. You and the parents will know whether the child needs to be taken to a vision specialist, the family physician, a specialist or a combination of these. Parents will have hard evidence/observation in hand from both school and home with which to approach the doctors. If more help is needed than the family doctor can provide, see Resources at the back of this book to locate a doctor of environmental medicine or a behavioral optometrist in your area. If parents are not satisfied with the doctor, they can try another.

Treatment of Problems

If the family physician prescribes antihistamines or a special diet, you, the teacher, will be able to note the effects on the child. This information will be helpful to the parents and will probably reinforce what the parents are observing at home. If the results are good, the parents and the child will benefit from hearing that. The child will experience increased self-esteem. If the results are not good, parents need to know that, too. Some areas of concern:

has the handwriting improved?
have letter reversals decreased or disappeared?
are assignments being completed?
is spelling better?
is the child less often louder than others?
is the child less clumsy, hyperactive or irritable?
is the child sleepy or dragging through the day?

If handwriting has improved and the child is exhibiting other positive signs but finding it difficult to stay awake, communicate this to the parents. The dosage of the antihistamines must be monitored and changed to reduce this effect. Some children have positive results with as little as an eighth of a tablet and then do not suffer from sleepiness.[51]

If a child has vision problems, improvement usually is seen in schoolwork and behavior within two weeks from the time the parents begin the vision training activities. In order to make good progress, activities must be performed for 15 minutes a day, 3-5 days a week. (The more frequent and the longer the time spent doing the vision training activities, the quicker the improvement.) Relay these results to the student and his parents.

Supposing the problem is both medical and visual —ideally the child will be started immediately on an elimination diet or antihistamines and will see a vision specialist and order vision training equipment right away. Teachers will usually see some improvement in the classroom within three days. By the second week, teachers often have a "different child" in the classroom. Two weeks from the time vision training activities are implemented, you will see even more improvement and the child will have an easier time both academically and behaviorally.

After having had several children move from the bottom reading or math group to the top group, a teacher may be ready to tell other teachers in the school about this program.

Part III
For Schools

The Whole School Approach

Vision

About 80 percent of all learning in the classroom is through the visual system. Schools employ audiologists to test children's hearing and speech therapists to teach students to say sounds correctly. If gross motor problems are apparent, schools hire physical therapists to correct those problems. Why not have schools equally obligated to teach children to focus, aim and move their eyes effectively? If vision performance interferes with learning and earning a living, why not have schools correct this?

It is generally accepted that about a third of high school graduates never read a book after graduation. Many students do not finish high school because they can not read for long periods of time, or they develop symptoms while reading. Even if they make it through high school, many do not go on to college. Many adults do not like to drive at night. Many turn down promotions and the opportunity to advance in careers because they do not like paperwork. These problems very likely relate to functional vision problems which could have been prevented or corrected in a few weeks (200 minutes) in a good school vision program; fortunately, such problems can still be corrected in adults.

In our research with over 2,000 students, with the use of the Performance-based Vision Stress Test, 53-56 percent of students in every classroom tested reported severe symptoms or got closer to their work than 8 inches. The symptoms these students experienced included dizziness, headaches or blurry vision. Students who get close to their work, even though they are unaware of the reason, usually do so to suppress the vision in one eye, thereby avoiding symptoms. Some of these students actually put their heads on their desk while working. To verify this with a student who gets too close to his/her work, place a red/green reading bar over the book, have the student wear red/green glasses and then read to you. The student will read only what is under one color on the reading bar (see p. 42 for information on equipment).

Colorado's Guidelines for School Vision Screening Programs (developed by Colorado optometrists, ophthalmologists, nurses and the State Department of Education) require any student who develops symptoms to be referred to a vision specialist.[52] Even if a student is referred, most optometrists and ophthalmologists only check to see if a person needs lenses. They do not check functional vision. Our research indicates lenses totally correct a scant 12 percent of problems. The vision training activities outlined in the parent section have suggestions for schools. The activities require an average of approximately 200 minutes (if the student is concentrating on the training activity) to correct most functional vision problems. At the end of this time, we have found that the student can move, aim and focus his or her eyes properly and will start reading for pleasure. Once the whole school has been screened and vision training activities have been completed with students who need them, only new students will subsequently need functional vision screening or training.

A Chance to Grow

Traditional remedial and special education programs may become unnecessary when students' basic vision and medical problems are dealt with appropriately. Research supporting this idea is available from A Chance To Grow, a corporation dedicated to accelerating the development of learning disabled, brain-injured and delayed children (these same methods will work on normal children who just need a little help). A Chance to Grow, at 3820 Emerson Avenue North, Minneapolis, Minnesota 54121 (612) 521-2266, is a kindergarten through eighth grade charter school. A behavioral optometrist works at the school three days a week. Students with medical problems are referred to member doctors of the American Academy of Environmental Medicine. A Chance to Grow willingly shares their research results. They have workshops and videos available to help train teachers and parents who wish to duplicate their program.

A recent study available from the OEP Foundation also supports this idea. "A Randomized Prospective Masked and Matched Comparative Study of Orthoptic Treatment Versus Conventional Reading Tutoring Treatment of Reading Disabilities in 62 Children," by D. Atzmon, C.O., P. Nemet, M.A., A. Ishay, Ph.D., and E. Karni, M.A., was published in 1991, and presented in March 1990 at the International Congress of Ophthalmology in Singapore.[53] The 62 children were divided into two groups: a remedial reading group and a vision training group. Both groups made significant gains. Follow-up studies indicate the remedial reading group regressed somewhat but still developed symptoms while the vision training group continued to improve in reading skills and were symptom-free.

A paper, "The Efficacy of Optometric Vision Therapy," in the February 1988 issue of the *Journal of the American Optometric Association* lists 238 studies which show that vision training can be used "for modifying and improving vision functioning." OEP Foundation has compiled a list (with over 2,000 papers by the mid-1990s) of all vision training research.

While norming the PVS Test and working in schools, Allan Crane discovered that most children with functional vision problems had learned to do abstract thinking (Piaget) to a much higher degree than the "top" students. They had been forced to think of ways to survive in the regular classroom and had become creative. When vision problems were corrected they often became the "top" group in the class. Teachers, can you imagine what a pleasure teaching would be and how much more you could teach if classes did not have "bottom" groups?

A program to improve vision functioning in your school can be implemented by dedicated, informed teachers and parents. You can share the information in this book with your parent-teacher organization or PTA and help have it adopted as a program in your school. Parents Active for Vision Education (P.A.V.E.) has available a vision resource library and a wonderful video and suggestions for guest speakers for school organizations.

Preventing Vision Problems

Prevention is always preferable to treatment. Schools can prevent some vision problems from developing or from becoming serious by using the following:

Desk Heights The distance from a child's eyes to the book or work surface should be 14 inches for young students and 16 inches for older students. If the desk height is less than 14 inches, you are putting the child under additional visual stress. Ideally, desks should slope 20 degrees so that the eyes do not have to change focus as the child reads down the page.

Templates The template program developed by the Lions Club in Winter Haven, Florida, is an excellent preventative program for pre-school, kindergarten and first grade. (The authors have even used templates with individual high school students in private situations). This particular Lions Club has over twenty-five years of research in the program.[54] Many children have spent most of their young lives 6-10 feet in front of a television set. Children do not have to change focus or move their eyes while watching television. When these children enter school they need to learn to focus, move and aim their eyes at near range: 14 inches. The template program helps with eye–hand coordination, eye movement, eye alignment and focusing skills especially at reading distance.

If a child has trouble learning the alphabet, has spelling problems and/or guesses at words, it may be due to a scanning problem. Children with a scanning problem do not know how to look at letters or words. There is no simple test for scanning. Most scanning problems can be virtually eliminated in six weeks through use of the template program.

In the past, the Bender Gestalt, Visual Motor Integration Test (VMI) and other perception tests based on the average age a child can draw circles, squares, diamonds and so on were widely used to label children and place them in special education. Many children were labeled brain damaged if they rotated four of these drawings. Problems found on a Bender Gestalt or VMI can be corrected in six weeks with the use of the Lions' template program.

Plastic templates are 8½ by 11 inches and contain a 2 inch circle, a square, a triangle, a diamond and rectangle (see the following). They are available from OEP Foundation (see the Resource section (p. 42) for the address; tel: 714-250-8070.)

The best results from template activities are achieved when a teacher actually performs the template activity with the students. The most effective arrangement is a group of up to eight students at a kidney shaped table.

To correct scanning and distortion of shape errors found on the VMI and Bender Gestalt, place the template on a sheet of paper. Have the student draw around each figure ten times with a pencil. Take the template off the paper and let the child trace around each figure on the paper five times with a light colored crayon. It is best to go counter clockwise and count while going around each figure. When drawing around the square, start at the top left hand corner and draw downward, saying "one" each time a corner of the square is touched. When the top left hand corner is touched again say "two." Continue around the square saying "two" each time a corner is touched. Repeat this exercise ten times. Count similarly when tracing with crayons.

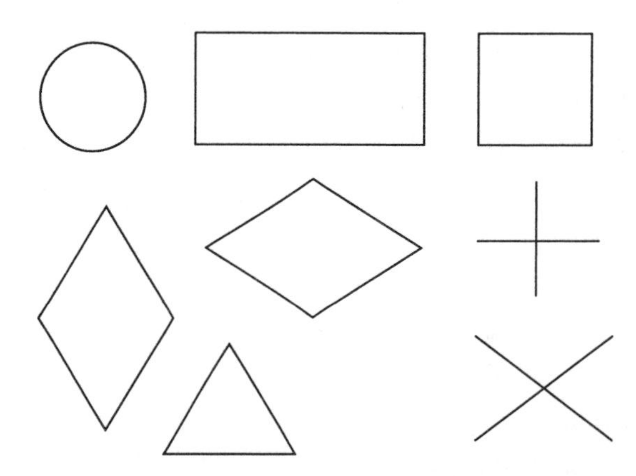

To correct integration, perseverance and rotation problems found on the VMI and Bender Gestalt, use the geometric shapes to make snow angels, robots, houses, rockets, stars, slinkies and so on. Stars can be made using squares, triangles and diamonds.

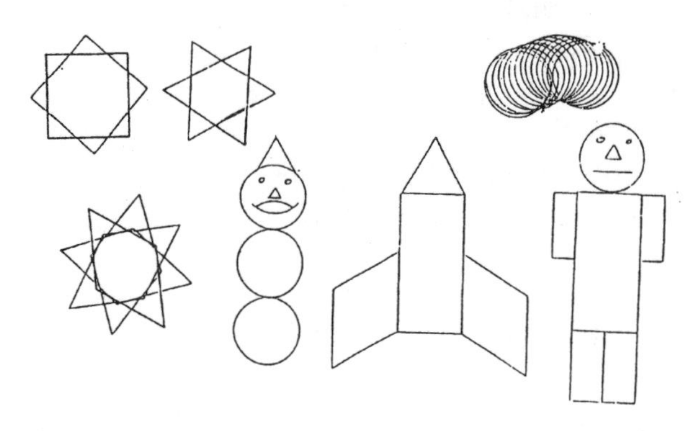

Guided Reader This is an excellent tool for teaching kindergarten students to recognize numbers and the alphabet. It also teaches correct eye movement, left to right, for reading. A filmstrip that has three numbers, letters or words per line is projected on a screen 10-20 feet away. Students count (or say) the numbers or letters for sixteen lines. Filmstrips with the common sight words are available for upper grade students. A whole classroom can be taught at one time. Children who have not yet learned the numbers, letters or words can see them from 10-20 feet away and not have to focus their eyes at near while they hear the material being read.

Sometimes students can not keep up with others in their classes because they mentally say every word they read. This limits them to about 125 words per minute. When a child has gone through the visual training activities and still reads slowly, use a guided reader system.

The old guided reader used in the 1960s and 1970s is a filmstrip projector that exposes one word at a time from left to right on a screen. Guided reading is now available on computer. The speed of the words appearing on screen or computer is gradually increased over time, thus helping students overcome the voicing barrier. When students read at least 175 words per minute with good comprehension, they can be successful in the classroom. **Guided reading on computers should not be used before remediating functional visual problems as it is too stressful.**

The following chart shows "Taylor's National Norms" for silent reading rate with 80 percent comprehension for each grade level.

Grade	Words Per Minute	Grade	Words Per Minute
1	80	7	195
2	115	8	204
3	138	9	214
4	158	10	224
5	173	11	237
6	185	12	250

See the Resource section in the back of this book for information on purchasing guided reading programs for each grade. (Some of the guided reader machines and filmstrips may be sitting unused in schoolroom closets or the media center, so check first.)

Correcting Vision Problems in Schools

Before starting vision training in your school, a commitment needs to be made to allow at least 10-15 minutes per day at least 3 days a week (5 is better). Weekly records must be kept of the progress of each student in each activity. A chart for this purpose is provided on p.45. The changes seen in students in the first two weeks of vision training will convince even reluctant and doubtful members of the staff of its value.

To make this process easier, the authors have produced a video to go with this book, detailing how to design and manage a home or school vision training program. This video (available from the OEP Foundation) shows the vision training activities and the role of the optometrist. Although not absolutely necessary, the video is very helpful.

A school vision program requires contracting with an optometrist to be a consultant and organizing volunteers or school staff to do the remediation. One parent or teacher coordinates the program to ensure its smooth running. Records are kept by volunteers or school staff. **If significant gains are not made, the child is immediately seen by the optometrist who comes to the school weekly.**

The PTA or PTO raises money to hire an optometrist. At the beginning of the program, the optometrist spends a few minutes with each child to evaluate if the student needs a complete eye examination and is a candidate for vision training activities. The optometrist does three tests: retinoscopy, eye alignment and acuity tests. The cost for an optometrist is about the same that schools pay an audiologist to check hearing. The vision specialist should be able to evaluate 350 students in two half days. A volunteer who knows the children's names is needed to record findings. **The school nurse, who is probably one of the busiest people in the school, is not a good choice for this; it is vital that the nurse continue to care for sick**

and hurt children and to coordinate the regular school vision screening and referral program as well as other screening programs.

Schools need the vision consultant weekly to evaluate those students who do not make significant gains in any of the areas of vision training. This takes about an hour a week for four to six weeks. At this time the optometrist will examine in detail any children who do not make significant gains in any of the areas of vision activities.

Sometimes grants can be obtained. A Chance to Grow may share pointers for getting grants. The OEP Foundation can provide research information that may help obtain grants. The logistics of a vision program in the school are relatively simple. The authors have used two different plans successfully. Parent volunteers are very effective in both these plans.

In Plan One, vision training activities are carried out in each classroom as the first activity in the morning while the regular classroom teacher is checking the attendance, doing lunch count and so on. These activities are under the direction of a parent volunteer or a teacher or other school personnel free of classroom duties during that period. Students work in pairs or groups on vision training activities.

In Plan Two, three parent volunteers go into one classroom. Each volunteer supervises the activities at one of three centers: eye movement, focusing and eye alignment. Students go to each volunteer for three minutes. The volunteers are in and out of the room in ten minutes before going to another classroom.

Vision Skills Necessary For School Success

Over 80 percent of what a child learns in school is through the visual system. We must teach children how to move their eyes, focus their eyes and aim them where they want to look. These skills must be taught under the direction of an optometrist. Weekly records must be kept. If there is a week in which a student does not make significant gains in all activities, that student must be referred to the consulting optometrist.

Minimum activities are in the Parent Section. The authors believe these activities are necessary to teach a child to move, aim and focus his eyes. Below each activity are suggestions for adapting the activity to a school setting. Our research shows these activities will help 70 percent of the students be symptom-free and **start reading for pleasure in four weeks.** In our experience, about 30 percent of the students labeled learning disabled, attention deficit disordered, attention deficit hyperactive disordered and students with special needs were moved out of special education after successfully completing these activities. The authors believe that when children begin to read for pleasure and are free of uncomfortable symptoms, they are ready to function effectively in school and life. **However, behavioral optometrists have many additional activities they can use to fine tune visual systems to a higher degree when these activities have been mastered, if parents desire.**

Students Who Need Additional Help After vision training, about 7 percent of the students will continue to develop symptoms. Helping these students requires a lot of teamwork between home, school and vision specialist. One of the tests these students need from the vision specialist is for aniseikonia[55] (one eye sees a larger image than the other eye). Aniseikonia is corrected with lenses. Textbooks say 3 percent of people have aniseikonia. When working with schools, I never fail to wonder which students have this problem. An excellent book for vision specialists on aniseikonia is *Clinical Management of Binocular Vision* by Mitchell Scheiman, O.D., and Bruce Wick, O.D., Ph.D. (available from the OEP Foundation).

The Vision Specialist

Vision specialists who offer vision training may be concerned about losing business when they work as school consultants. Helping the school with students who continue to develop symptoms after completing school vision training and doing vision training with students who have complex vision problems with which the school can not work will keep these practitioners more than busy.

Some 5-10 percent of students have problems so complex they can not be helped by a school vision program. These students will have to be referred for in-office diagnosis and vision training by a vision specialist at the parents' expense. Lions' Clubs and other service clubs may help needy families with this expense; health insurance may cover it. Vision specialists will work in their offices with students whose eyes are turned or crossed or have been cosmetically corrected by surgery. Vision specialists will have to work with students with amblyopia (at least two lines difference in acuity between the two eyes). Students with certain types of eye movement problems (nystagmus, oculomotor apraxia) and/or students with aniseikonia will also continue working directly with vision specialists.

The norms and standards proposed here are different from those of most vision specialists. **Every child should be able to move, aim, and focus his/her eyes efficiently before being placed under educational stress and before being *labeled.*** When the authors worked with students, it became obvious that it is imperative to do vertical eye alignment activities with students before or at the same time as other activities. By doing vertical eye alignment activities at the beginning and to the specifications in this book, the time necessary for correcting vision problems is cut in half.

Without a school vision program, many children are denied access to adequate vision care for various reasons including distance, expense, awareness and local knowledge. The authors are interested in all students succeeding in school and in life. Some honor students will have an easier time and be more efficient after developing good vision skills. While better vision skills can not correct Down's Syndrome or brain damage, they may be used to make the lives of some of these children easier and more productive.[56] Some children are plagued by multiple difficulties.

The Future Of School Vision Programs

We need people in our schools who are trained to teach students to focus, aim their eyes and move their eyes smoothly and efficiently for effective information processing. The rewards in time saved and talents nurtured will be enormous.

It is possible to develop a certification program in colleges of optometry in conjunction with colleges of education to certify existing teachers to do vision training in schools under the direction of a consulting optometrist in the community. Even if school nurses do the vision screenings, usually they are so busy they do not have time to supervise vision training activities. The authors recommend that physical education teachers or special education resource teachers become the vision training activities expert in the school. They could work directly with groups of children in vision training and in preventative programs and/or work with classroom teachers or volunteers to carry out the programs.

Medical

The PTA or other parent-teacher group can help parents and teachers become aware of the medical aspects of learning and behavior problems by making this book and the books and videos in the reference section available and presenting the information at PTA or public meetings. The parent-teacher group may also invite local doctors who are members of the American Association of Environmental Medicine (AAEM) to speak (AAEM, #10 Randolph St., New Hope, PA 18938, (215) 862-4574).

Parents and teachers might investigate the possibility of pollutants in their school. In her book *The Impossible Child In School At Home,* Doris Rapp, M.D., has excellent sections with suggestions for teachers, in-service for school conferences and suggestions for parent-teacher conferences. Another important consideration is the possibility of eliminating MSG from the school lunch program. Since allergies affect about 70 percent of school children,[57] the PTA could research (see menus by Drs. Rapp and Crook) and develop a program to provide foods for children on special diets. The AAEM may be a helpful source of information and suggestions (see above.)

In addition to the basic vision and medical programs, parent-teacher groups can sponsor or encourage programs such as Jump Rope for Heart. Fancy, fast jump rope programs may be an alternative to antihistamines in some cases. The Jump for Heart Program when executed expertly is terrific. Newell Kephart, Ph.D., a pioneer in special education, emphasizes gross motor activities.[58] Dr. Kephart inspired the Winter Haven Lions Club template program when he gave a talk on eye hand coordination at one of their luncheons. Dance and gymnastics are great rhythmic activities which help many children. Margaret Sasse has 38 very successful Toddler Kindy Gymbaroo Schools in Australia which specialize in gross motor activities.[59]

A Chance to Grow Charter School, which began by taking high-risk kindergarteners from the Minneapolis, Minnesota, school system for an hour a day, has a great track record for motor activities as well as vision training and environmental medical referrals. By the end of third grade, instead of being retained these students were in the top third of the class. Do these physical activities increase endorphins so there is improved firing across brain cells? More research is needed, but these are all worthwhile activities. The authors have had many children become successful in school after their involvement with Jump Rope For Heart programs. Rhythmic activities seem to help children. When teaching, the authors have seen great improvement in some children's academic achievement after they became proficient at the game of jacks, which involves vision and eye–hand coordination.

Opportunities For Research

Are the minimum vision activities described here enough to help students work to their full potential? Are additional activities needed? These are questions some optometrists will have. It was decided these activities were sufficient because most children with whom the authors worked started reading for pleasure after completing the activities outlined in the previous pages.

If the parent from whom the child inherited vision problems does vision training activities with the child, by how much is the time required to correct the child's problem reduced? Do adults who have had eye surgery to straighten their eyes as children have a depth-perception problem? Does this lead to higher accident rates and insurance premiums?

You might want to try a biofeedback program developed by ADHD (at 6100 Ventura Boulevard, Ste. 10, Encino, CA 91436) which appears to have the same results as the guided reader. The individual (child or adult) looks at a Pac Man game on a computer screen. An electrode which is fed into a biofeedback machine is connected to the top of the player's head. When the player concentrates, Pac Man is bright and moves swiftly; when the player is not concentrating, Pac Man moves slowly and is dim. The aim of this biofeedback is to improve the individual's ability to concentrate and thus decrease behavior often referred to as hyperactivity or attention deficit disorder. Naturally, this also decreases personal frustration levels and enables one to work more effectively. Over one hundred centers in the U.S. have this equipment.

Do such activities train the two visual pathways (reported by Gracia, et al) to work together? Why does Ritalin appear to relieve a functional vision problem? Dr. William Ludlum at Pacific University has done research on the alpha brain wave and learning. People who can not suppress alpha do not have good comprehension when they read. Does Ritalin suppress alpha? Does Ritalin allow a person to suppress alpha? Does Ritalin allow the suppression of one of the two vision pathways? Does Ritalin merely control youngsters so that they are not problems?

Compare juvenile delinquency, time served in jail, addiction to drugs and educational achievement of students who received Ritalin with those who received Nystatin and/or diet and/or vision training.

Why does vigorous exercise help people think and do better academically? Do vigorous exercises change brain chemistry so the firing from cell to cell is improved? Exercise appears to work in place of antihistamines and Ritalin in some cases. Jump Rope For Heart activities, song and dance routines, competitive swimming, crawling and moving activities are advocated by some individuals. What effect will the elimination of music and physical education programs have upon student learning?

Do the crawling and creeping activities done at A Chance to Grow program train the eyes to work together as a team? Will the eye training activities advocated in this book have the same results? Do parents need to be cautioned about the use of baby walkers, which stifle a child's crawling activities?

Students who can do two base up and base down and six base in and out eye activities often read for pleasure. Do Dr. Levinson's patients who are treated for middle ear problems also read for pleasure? Do any Ritalin patients start reading for pleasure? Students who can move, aim and focus their eyes well have good binocular vision. Our research shows it does not matter with these students if they are cross dominate (right handed and left eyed or left handed and right eyed). Does it matter about right and left brain activities?

Research into such topics would be invaluable.

Appendix

Endnotes

1. Flach, F., *Rickie.* New York, N.Y.: Ballantine Books, 1991.

2. Callahan, M., *Fighting For Tony.* New York, N.Y.: Simon & Schuster, 1987. pp. 44-45.

3. Ibid.

4. Ibid., p. 8.

5. Rapp, D., *Is This Your Child?* New York, N.Y.: William Morrow & Co., 1991. pp. 33-34.

6. Crook, W. G., L. Stevens, *Solving the Puzzle of Your Hard-to-Raise Child.* New York, N.Y.: Random House, 1987. pp. 47-48.

7. Taylor, S. E., H. Frackenpohl, and J. L. Pette, "Grade Level Norms for the Components of the Fundamental Reading Skill," EDL Research Information Bulletin No. 3, Educational Developmental Laboratories, Inc. Thirty-nine colleges and universities were involved in this research.

8. Rapp, D., *The Impossible Child.* Buffalo, N.Y.: Practical Allergy Research Foundation, 1989. pp. 7, 10, 12, 18, 19, 20, 22, 27.

9. Rapp, D., *The Impossible Child.* Buffalo, N.Y.: Practical Allergy Research Foundation.

10. Flach, F., *Rickie.* New York, N.Y.: Ballantine Books, 1991.

11. Ibid., p. 244.

12. Crook, W. G., L. Stevens, *Solving the Puzzle of Your Hard-to-Raise Child.* New York, N.Y.: Random House, 1987. pp. 12-15.

13. Crook, W. G., *Help For The Hyperactive Child.* Jackson, TN.: Professional Books, 1991. pp. 101-115.

14. Levinson, H. N., *Smart But Feeling Dumb.* New York, N.Y.: Warner Books, Inc., 1984.

15. Levinson, H. N., *Total Concentration.* New York, N.Y.: M. Evans & Co., 1990.

16. Dawkins, H. R., E. Edelman, C. Forkiotis, *The Suddenly Successful Student.* (lst edition, 1986) now available from OEP Foundation, Santa Ana, CA.: p. 37.

17. Dawkins, H. R., E. Edelman, C. Forkiotis, *The Suddenly Successful Student.* (3rd edition, 1990). OEP Foundation, Santa Ana, CA.: p. 43.

18. Crane, A.D., B. Wick, *Crane-Wick Vision and Hearing Efficiency Test.* Santa Ana, CA.: OEP Foundation, 1987.

19. *Guidelines for School Vision Screening Programs,* September 1991. Developed by the Colorado School Vision Screening Interdisciplinary Task Force (consisting of ophthalmologists, optometrists, school nurses), Colorado Health Department, Boces, Colorado Department of Education.

20. Rusk, J., Murry, *A Visual Screening Program for Unit II,* Charlottetown, Prince Edward Island, Canada: 1992.

21. Malzow, M. L., T. D. France, S. Finkleman, J. Frank, P. Jenkins, "Acute Accommodative and Convergence Insufficiency," *Tr. Amer. Ophth. Soc.,* Vol. LXXXVIII, 1989.

22. Boorish, I. M., *Clinical Refraction,* 3rd edition, Chicago, IL.: The Professional Press, Inc., 1970. p. 869.

23. Scheiman, M., B. Wick, *Clinical Management of Binocular Vision.* Philadelphia, PA.: J. B. Lippincott Co., 1994. pp. 40-41.

24. Ibid., pp. 1-13.

25. Rapp, D., *The Impossible Child.* Buffalo, N.Y.: Practical Allergy Research Foundation, 1989. p. xii.

26. Ibid., p. 74.

27. Crook, W. G., L. Stevens, *Solving the Puzzle of Your Hard-to-Raise Child.* New York, N.Y.: Random House, Inc., 1987. pp. 47-52.

28. Levinson, H. N., *Smart But Feeling Dumb.* New York, N.Y.: Warner Books, Inc. 1984. pp. 1-10.

29. Levinson, H. N., *Total Concentration*, New York, N.Y.: M. Evans & Co., 1990. pp. 10-11.

30. Rapp, D., *The Impossible Child.* Buffalo, N.Y.: Practical Allergy Research Foundation, pp. 74-78.

31. Rapp, D., *Is This Is Your Child?* New York, N.Y.: William Morrow & Co., 1991. pp. 228-232.

32. Ibid., p. 35.

33. Crook, W. G., *Help for Your Hyperactive Child.* Jackson, TN.: Professional Books, 1991. pp. 170-174.

34. Schwartz, G. R., *In Bad Taste: The MSG Syndrome.* New York, N.Y.: Penguin Group, 1990.

35. Blaylock, R. L. , *Excitotoxins: The Taste That Kills.* Santa Fe, N.M.: Health Press, 1994. p. 216.

36. Rapp, D., *Is This Your Child?* New York, N.Y.: William Morrow & Co., 1991. pp. 157-71.

37. Crook, W. G., L. Steven, *Solving the Puzzle of Your Hard-to-Raise Child.* New York, N.Y.: Random House, Inc., 1987. p. 96.

38. Rapp, D., *The Impossible Child.* Buffalo, N.Y.: Practical Allergy Research Foundation, 1989. pp. 74-84.

39. Crook, W. G., L. Stevens, *Solving the Puzzle of Your Hard-to-Raise Child.* New York, N. Y.: Random House, Inc., 1987. pp. 48-52.

40. Rapp, D., *The Impossible Child.* Buffalo, N.Y.: Practical Allergy Research Foundation, 1989. pp. 7-39.

41. Rapp, D., *Is This Your Child?* New York, N.Y.: William Morrow & Co., 1991. p. 35.

42. Levinson, H. N., *Smart But Feeling Dumb.* New York, N.Y.: Warner Books, Inc., 1984. p. 35.

43. Crook, W. G., *Help for the Hyperactive Child.* Jackson. TN.: Professional Books, 1991. pp. 233-38.

44. Blaylock, R. L., *Excitotoxins: The Taste That Kills.* Santa Fe, N.M.: Health Press. 1994. pp. 215-16.

45. Ibid., p. 71.

46. Ibid., pp. 80-82.

47. Shwartz, G. R., *In Bad Taste: The MSG Syndrome.* New York, N.Y.: Penguin Group, 1990. p. 19.

48. Blaylock, R. L., *Excitotoxins: The Taste That Kills.* Santa Fe, N.M.: Health Press, 1994. p. 223.

49. Schwartz, G. R. *In Bad Taste: The MSG Syndrome.* New York, N.Y.: Penguin Group, 1990. pp. 97-107.

50. Ibid., pp. 109-114.

51. Levinson, H. N., *Smart But Feeling Dumb.* New York, N.Y.: Warner Books, Inc., 1984. p. 35.

52. *Guidelines for School Vision Screening Programs,* September 1991. Developed by the Colorado School Vision Screening Task Force (consisting of ophthalmologists, optometrists, school nurses); Colorado Department of Health, Boces, Colorado Department of Education.

53. Atzman, D., P. Nemet, A. Ishay, E. Karni, "A Randomized Prospective Masked and Matched Comparative Study of Orthoptic Treatment Versus Conventional Reading Tutoring Treatment for Reading Disabilities in 62 Children," *Binocular Vision & Eye Muscle Surgery Qrtly.,* Spring 1993, vol. 8 (No. 2): pp. 91-106.

54. Curry, G. I., *Winter Haven's Perceptual Testing and Training Handbook.* Winter Haven, FL.: Winter Haven Lions Research Foundation, Inc., 1969.

55. Scheiman, M., B. Wick, *Clinical Management of Binocular Vision.* Philadelphia, PA.: J. B. Lippincott Co., 1994. pp. 543-577.

56. Suchoff, I. B., G. T. Petito, "The Efficacy of Visual Therapy: Accommodative Disorders and Non-Strabismic Anomalies of Binocular Vision," *Journal of the American Optometric Association*, February 1986.

57. Rapp, D., *Is This Your Child?* New York, N.Y.: William Morrow & Co., 1991. p. 33.

58. Kephart, N. C., *The Slow Learner In the Classroom.* Columbus, Ohio: Merrill, 1960.

59. Sasse, M., *If Only We'd Known.* Kew, Victoria, Australia: Toddler Kindy Gymbaroo Pty Ltd., 1990.

Glossary of Terms

Accommodation The act of the lens of the eye adjusting to become flat at distance and curved near so that objects can be seen clearly at various distances.

Acuity Sharpness of vision.

Amblyopia Decreased visual acuity (usually only in one eye) not correctable by glasses and not caused by an apparent eye disease.

Binocularity The ability of the eyes to work together as a "team" in order to have depth perception.

Convergence The ability to turn the two eyes towards each other to look at a near object.

Eye–hand coordination The ability for the eye and hand to coordinate during a specific action such as handwriting or copying from the chalkboard.

Phoria The tendency for a horizontal or vertical misalignment of the two eyes.

Scanning The ability of the eyes to look at or between letters or word and groups of words and gain information. Children without this skill tend to guess at words and have a hard time learning the alphabet.

Saccadic Eye Movement Eye movements that occur between words or groups of words during reading; each fixation averages one forth second.

Snellen Chart Chart used to measure acuity at a specific distance (usually 10 or 20 feet).

Strabismus Failure of each eye to fixate on an object at the same time. One eye fixes on an object and the other turns away (either in, esotropia, or out, exotropia).

Suppression The suspension of the visual information of one eye when both eyes should be used.

Visual Perception The interpretation of visual information and integration of the information with the other senses and past experience.

Suggested Reading

Blaylock, R. L., *Excitotoxins: The Taste That Kills.* Santa Fe, N.M.: Health Press, 1994.

Curry, G. I. *Winter Haven's Perceptual Testing and Training Handbook.* Winter Haven, Florida: Winterhaven Lions Research Foundation, Inc., 1969.

Crook, W. G., *Help for the Hyperactive Child.* Jackson, TN.: Professional Books, 1991.

Crook, W. G., and L. Stevens, *Solving the Puzzle of Your Hard-to-Raise Child.* New York, N.Y.: Random House Inc., 1987.

Dawkins, H. R., E. Edelman, C. Forkiotis, *Suddenly Successful.* OEP Foundation, Santa Ana, CA.: 1991.

Dawkins, H. R., E. Edelman, C. Forkiotis, *The Suddenly Successful Student.* OEP Foundation, Santa Ana, CA.: 1991.

Flach, F., *Rickie.* New York, NY: Ballantine Books, 1991.

Philpott, W. H., B. K. Kalita, *Brain Allergies.* New Canaan, CT.: Keats Publishing, 1986.

Levinson, H. N., *Smart But Feeling Dumb.* New York, N.Y.: Warner Books Inc., 1984.

Levinson, H .N., *Total Concentration.* New York, N.Y.: M. Evans & Co., 1990.

Rapp, R. J., *Is This Your Child?* New York, N.Y.: William Morrow & Co., 1991.

Rapp, R. J., *The Impossible Child.* Practical Allergy Research Foundation, P.O. Box 60, Buffalo, N.Y.: 14223. 1989.

Sasse, M., *If Only We'd Known.* Kew, Victoria, Australia: Toddler Kindy Gymbaroo Pty Ltd., 1990.

Scheiman, M., B. Wick, *Clinical Management of Binocular Vision.* Philadelphia, PA.: J. B. Lippincott Co., 1994.

Schwartz, G. R., *In Bad Taste: The MSG Syndrome.* New York, N.Y.: Penguin Group, 1990.

Resources

FOR INFORMED MEDICAL CARE

American Academy of Environmental Medicine
#10 Randolph Street
New Hope, PA 18938
(215) 862-4544/4574

FOR INFORMED VISION CARE

American Academy of Optometry
Section of Binocular Vision & Perception
5530 Wisconsin Avenue NW, Suite 917
Washington, DC 20815

College of Optometrists in Visual Development
353 H Street, Suite C
Chula Vista, CA 92010

Optometric Extension Program Foundation
1921 Carnegie Ave.
Suite # 3 L
Santa Ana, CA 92705
(714) 250-8070

P.A.V.E.
(Parents Active For Vision Education)
9620 Chesapeake Drive
San Diego, CA 92123
1-800 PAVE 988

"Founded in 1988, P.A.V.E. is a nonprofit educational organization committed to raising national awareness about the importance of total visual health as it effects achievement in life. P.A.V.E.'s mission was inspired by the personal experiences of our families and students as they struggled with the effects of undetected learning related vision problems."

FOR VISION TRAINING EQUIPMENT

Gulden Optical
P.O. Box 7154
Elkins Park, PA 19027
(800) 659-2250

OEP Foundation
1921 Carnegie Avenue
Suite #3L
Santa Ana, CA 92705
(714) 250-8070
OEP has kits available to go with the exercises in *Buzzards to Bluebirds.*

GTVT
17907 25th Dr. SE
Bothell, Washington, 98012
1-800 848-8897

Bernell Corporation
422 East Monroe Street
South Bend, Indiana, 46601

FOR COMPUTER-GUIDED READER PROGRAMS

Taylor and Associates
200-2E. Second Street
Huntington Station, New York 11746
1-800-732-3758

FOR EDUCATIONAL INFORMATION

A Chance to Grow/New Visions School
112 19th Ave. N.E.
Minneapolis, Minnesota 54121,
(612) 521-2266.

Dr. William G. Crook's Elimination Diet
Detecting Hidden Food Allergies (HFA)

Although skin tests help physicians identify allergies to ragweed, grasses, dust mites and animal danders, such tests provide little help in detecting hidden food allergies (HFA).

Common signs and symptoms in both adults and children with HFA include fatigue, pass, congestion, dark circles under their eyes, headache, muscle aches, irritability, abdominal pain, hyperactivity, attention deficits, memory loss and other problems. In discussing food sensitivities, Art Ulene, M.D., said: "An elimination diet, properly conducted, is a very reasonable and practical way to identify foods that are causing problems."

Carrying out a diet isn't easy. It takes careful planning. Here are some of the things you'll need to do in order to succeed:

1. Before beginning your trial diet, discuss it with members of your family.
2. Carry out the diet at an appropriate time. (Don't try it during a holiday.)
3. Before beginning a diet, keep a diary or symptom inventory for at least 3 days.
4. Continue the symptom diary while you're following the diet.
5. On the initial elimination diet, you and your child can eat the following foods:
   a. any vegetable but corn
   b. any meat but bacon, sausage, hot dogs and luncheon meat
   c. rice, oats, barley and the grain alternatives, amaranth, quinoa and buckwheat (available at health food stores)
   d. any fruit but citrus (also avoid any fruit you eat more than once a week)
   e. bottled, spring or distilled water and herb teas.
6. On the initial elimination diet you and your child should avoid:

milk	egg	sugar
tea	peas	wheat
coffee	beans	peanuts
Kool-aid	corn	chocolate
soft drinks	processed foods	food colors and dyes

7. Continue the diet for 5 to 10 days, until there is convincing improvement in your symptoms lasting 48 hours.
8. Then to identify food troublemakers, the eliminated foods should be eaten again (one food per day) and reactions should be noted. (Symptoms may be noticed within a few minutes or they may not appear for several hours or until the next day.)

Special Note: If you have been bothered by asthma, severe hives, swelling or other serious allergy reactions, consult your physician before carrying out this diet.

Weekly Progress Charts

Name: ______________________________

Activity	Week 1	Week 2	Week 3	Week 4	Week 5	Week 6

Name: ______________________________

Activity	Week 1	Week 2	Week 3	Week 4	Week 5	Week 6

Name: ______________________________

Activity	Week 1	Week 2	Week 3	Week 4	Week 5	Week 6

Weekly Progress Charts

Name: ______________________________

Activity	Week 1	Week 2	Week 3	Week 4	Week 5	Week 6

Name: ______________________________

Activity	Week 1	Week 2	Week 3	Week 4	Week 5	Week 6

Name: ______________________________

Activity	Week 1	Week 2	Week 3	Week 4	Week 5	Week 6

Educator's Guide to Classroom Vision Problems

Student's
Name ____________________________ Date ______
Age ______________ Grade __________________

1. Appearance of Eyes:

__ One eye turns in or out at any time
__ Reddened eyes or lids
__ Eyes tear excessively
__ Encrusted eyelids
__ Frequent styes of lids

2. Complaints when using eyes at desk:

__ Headaches in forehead or temples
__ Burning or itching after reading or desk work
__ Nausea or dizziness
__ Print blurs after reading a short time

3. Behavioral Signs of Visual Problems:

A. Eye Movement Abilities (Ocular Motility)

__ Head turns as reads across page
__ Loses place often during reading
__ Needs finger or marker to keep place
__ Displays short attention span in reading or copying
__ Too frequently omits words
__ Repeatedly omits "small" words
__ Writes up or down hill on paper
__ Rereads or skips lines unknowingly
__ Orients drawings poorly on page

B. Eye Teaming Abilities (Binocularity)

__ Complains of seeing double (diplopia)
__ Repeats letters within words
__ Omits letter, numbers or phrases
__ Misaligns digits in number columns
__ Squints, closes or covers one eye
__ Tilts head extremely while working at desk
__ Consistently shows gross postural deviations at all desk activities

C. Eye-Hand Coordinations Abilities

__ Must feel of things to assist in any interpretation required
__ Eyes not used to "steer" hand movements (extreme lack of orientation, placement of words or drawings on page)
__ Writes crookedly, poorly spaced: cannot stay on ruled lines
__ Misaligns both horizontal and vertical series of numbers
__ Uses a hand or finger(s) to keep the place on the page
__ Repeatedly confuses left-right directions

D. Visual Form Perception (Visual Comparison, Visual Imagery, Visualization)

__ Mistakes words with same or similar beginnings
__ Fails to recognize same word in next sentence
__ Reverses letters and/or words in writing and copying
__ Confuses likenesses and minor differences
__ Confuses same word in same sentence
__ Repeatedly confuses similar beginnings and endings of words
__ Fails to visualize what is read either silently or orally
__ Whispers to self for reinforcement while reading silently
__ Returns to "drawing with fingers" to decide likes and differences

E. Refractive Status (Nearsightedness, Farsightedness, Focus Problems, etc.)

__ Comprehension reduces as reading continued: loses interest too quickly
__ Mispronounces similar words as continues reading
__ Blinks excessively at desk tasks and/or reading; not elsewhere
__ Holds book too closely; face too close to desk surface
__ Avoids all possible near-centered tasks
__ Complains of discomfort in tasks that demand visual interpretation
__ Closes or covers one eye when reading or doing desk work
__ Makes errors in copying from reference book to notebook
__ Squints to see chalkboard, or requests to move nearer
__ Rubs eyes during or after short periods of visual activity
__ Fatigues easily; blinks to make chalkboard clear up after desk task
__ Observer's Suggestions

Signed (Print) ___________________________

Visual Function Self Test

Student's
Name ______________________ Date ______
Age ____________ Grade ______________

The following questions cover the most common symptoms optometrists observe in their patients. If you experience one or more of the problems on the list, it may be time to contact a behavioral optometrist. Take this self test with you on your first appointment. The results will help with the assessment of your visual problem.

Yes No

☐ ☐ Do you wear glasses for your reading?

☐ ☐ Do you enjoy reading?

☐ ☐ Do you think you should be able to read faster?

☐ ☐ Do you understand what you read as well as you'd like?

☐ ☐ Is it an effort to maintain your concentration while reading? (Short attention span)

☐ ☐ Do you tend to skip words or lines of print while reading?

☐ ☐ After reading, do you look up and notice that distant objects are momentarily blurred?

☐ ☐ Does print tend to appear blurry after reading for awhile?

☐ ☐ Do your eyes itch, burn, water, pull or ache? (Circle the problems you experience)

☐ ☐ Do you ever experience double vision while reading?

Yes No

☐ ☐ Do words appear to float or move while reading?

☐ ☐ Do you tend to lose your place while reading or copying?

☐ ☐ Do you tend to use your finger or a marker to keep your place while reading or copying?

☐ ☐ Do you have to re-read words or lines while reading?

☐ ☐ Do your eyes feel tired at the end of the day?

☐ ☐ Do you sometimes have to squint, close or cover one eye when reading?

☐ ☐ Do you ever experience headaches during or after reading?

☐ ☐ Are you especially sensitive to sunlight or glare?

☐ ☐ Are you aware of any tendency to move your head closer to, or away from what you are reading?

☐ ☐ If you use a computer, does the screen (VDT) bother your eyes?

______ How long can you read before you are aware of your eyes getting tired?

______ How many hours daily do you spend at a desk, or reading, or at other arm's length vision distances?

Crane Words

Primary	*First*	*Second*	*Third*	*Fourth*	*Fifth*	*Sixth*
is	came	across	forget	admit	melody	importance
the	what	large	against	grind	loyal	threat
we	under	river	child	pain	program	plunder
look	could	brother	whole	silence	musical	poultry
go	after	happen	awake	disturb	dignity	manager
baby	brown	friendly	flowers	forehead	limb	wealth
can	funny	sheep	stream	flight	perfume	location
down	was	eyes	island	anger	cough	radiator
up	dog	farmer	bench	blood	merchant	industry
blue	there	follow	daughter	hunger	homestead	wrench
in	girl	afternoon	damp	honest	semester	investigate
ball	work	beautiful	knife	weigh	promptly	source
get	then	beside	excuse	develop	crumble	graduate
you	laugh	field	beauty	reindeer	league	fringe
run	must	remember	enjoy	distant	minister	unexpected
come	very	great	half	million	wrist	recipe
ride	duck	table	yesterday	speechless	extended	monument
said	are	breakfast	reward	rough	review	varnish
by	name	middle	feast	claimed	operate	indicate
mother	doll	above	block	ordinary	pleasure	substitute

Performance-based Vision Stress Test

Performance-based Vision Stress Test

Parents or teachers may wish to use an instrument which has been normed and standardized for comparing a child's performance to other children of the same grade level. The Performance-based Vision Stress Test has been included here as such an instrument. The PVS Test was developed in 1987. This test does the same thing for vision that the treadmill stress test does for the heart. Each reveals how we perform under stress situations similar to those faced in our lives day by day.

Until 1987, there were reading tests and there were vision tests. If you wanted to find out how a child's vision affected his reading, the child had to read. So while you were testing functional vision skills, you were also testing phonic skills, sight word vocabulary and comprehension. It was extremely difficult to know if there was a reading problem or a vision problem. The only knowledge necessary for taking the PVS Test is numbers to five or the alphabet. It tests the vision skills necessary for school success without involving reading skills, and it tests these skills for a realistic period of time.

This vision stress test was normed on over 2,000 kindergarten to twelfth grade students in six states. We now know how much visual work an efficient student in each grade level should be able to complete while copying from the board, looking from word to word and while doing prolonged eye teaming (reading) in an established amount of time without developing symptoms.

Kindergarten through third grade students work with numbers up to five. Fourth grade and older students work with the alphabet. The test may be given to a whole class, a family or one child at a time.

Test Description: Kindergarten-Third Grade The test is divided into three parts: (1) near-far copy test: copying from chalkboard, (2) saccadic eye movement test: looking from word to word and (3) prolonged eye teaming test: reading. These tests and charts may be copied for private use, or the manual and test booklets may be purchased from the OEP Foundation (see Resources). You will need a watch with a second hand or a stopwatch for giving the test.

The complete test must be given at one time. The child's eyes should be 14 inches from the test booklet. For young children, a kitchen table is too high. A card table or properly adjusted school desk is much better.

Kindergarten-Third grade

Part A: Near-Far Copying

A chart is placed on the wall. On the chart, numbers appear in groups of three. The 20/20 charts come in two sizes: one for a distance of 10 feet; one for 20 feet. If you are testing a whole class, the larger charts are placed around the room so that each child can look directly at a chart 20 feet away. Students' desks are turned so that each student can see one of the charts at the correct distance. In a classroom you may have as many as ten charts. In homes, the small chart 10 feet from the child is usually more appropriate.

Part A: Directions. Say, **"Open your test booklet and fill out the information at the top of the page. Name, grade, age and date. Do you have glasses? Where did you get them? Are you wearing them today?"**

Say, **"Look at your paper. Put your finger on the A by the boxes under your name. I want you to**

copy as many of these numbers as you can in one minute. Put three numbers in each box. Go across the page. Does everyone know what you are going to do? Do not erase. On your mark, get set, go." Time the students for one minute. Then say, **"Stop, put your pencils down."**

Part B: Saccadic Eye Movement—practice looking from word to word. This activity is designed to evaluate how efficiently a student can look from number to number simulating the act of looking from word to word in reading. This is a practice section for activities in Parts C, D and F. Students will be working with numbers. Numbers are variously grouped in one's, two's or three's.

Sample
23 431 453 214 521 21 425 143 125 312 421 235

Part B: Directions. Say, **"This is a practice section. Look at the B on your paper. Notice what has been done. A line was drawn under the numbers. Continue drawing this line, and when you come to the first 1 circle it. Go on to the first 2 and circle it. What will we do next? Right, we will go to the 3 and circle it. Does everyone get the idea? Let's practice and go until we get to 5."**

When everyone has completed the practice line and understands the activity, say, **"Go to the next line. Start over with 1 each time you begin a new line. Draw a line under the numbers until you get to the first 1. Circle it. Go on to the first 2 and circle it. What will we do next? Right, we will go to the 3 and circle it. The numbers have been written at the top of each page for you to look at if you get the numbers mixed up. Go until you get to 5 on each line. Does anyone have any questions? Keep practicing until you get to "stop" at the bottom of the page. Does anyone have any questions about what we are doing?"**

Say, **"Please turn the page. Put your finger on the letter C. Go as far as you can in one minute with the same activity you have been doing. Do as many lines as you can. Any questions? Start over with 1 each time you begin a new line. Do not erase. Ready, go."**

Time the students for one minute. Say **"Stop, turn to the next page."** Do not let the students rest their eyes. Keep them doing the same activity in Part D.

Part D: Prolonged Eye Teaming - Reading.

At this stage, students will do the same activity they did in parts B and C at this time for ten minutes. With this activity we are evaluating eye alignment, binocularity, eye movement, focus, fusion, vergence and acuity under stress. This activity simulates reading but is much more difficult than actual reading because the student has to look at each number.

In order to compare amounts of work done in the first and second five minute time blocks, children will make a big X where they are working at the five minute time interval.

Part D: Directions. Say, **"We are going to keep doing the same activity we have been doing. Please turn the page. See the D. You will start working there. Turn the page and look at the next pages. They are the same activity with numbers at the top of each page. You will do this activity until I say stop."** (2 pages for kindergarten and first grade, three pages or to line 76 for second and third grade.) **"If you finish, raise your hand and I will give you additional pages. Do not stop working. Remember, you will do the same thing you did in parts 1 and 2. We want to see how much work you can do in 10 minutes. When you have been working 5 minutes, I will tell you to mark the place you are working with a big X this size."** (Show the children your fingers an X sized about ½ inch). **"Put your finger on the D again. We are ready to start the activity. Go as far as you can. Any questions? Do not erase. Ready, go."**

Record the starting time. Make notes on the test booklet of those children who get close to their work (8 inches or less), tilt their heads, rub their eyes, cover one eye, have watery eyes or squint. This is very important as children get close to their work and tilt their heads so they can suppress the vision in one eye, thus avoiding symptoms. These children usually have poor eye alignment.

Time the students for ten minutes. Say **"Stop, turn to the next page."** Do not let the students rest their eyes.

Part E: Copying From a Distance: Fatigue Check.

Part E is the same as Part A. Children copy as many letters or numbers as they can in one minute. This is to see if there is a fatigue factor.

Part E: Directions. Say, **"Put your finger on the E. I want you to copy as many of these numbers as you can in one minute. Put three numbers in each box. Go across the page. This is the same activity that you did in Part A. Does everyone know what you are going to do? Do not erase. On your mark, get set, go."** Time the students for one minute. Then say, **"Stop, put your pencils down."**

Part F: Saccadics: Fatigue Check

Part F is the same as Part C. This section evaluates how many lines of work students can do in 1 minute after having used their eyes for about 20 minutes. Was there a fatigue factor?

Part F: Directions. Say, **"Put your finger on the F. Children, you will do the same thing you did in Parts B, C and D for one minute. Do not erase. Do as many lines as you can. Any questions? Ready, go."**

Time the students for 1 minute. Then say, **"Stop."**

Immediately after students finish the test:

Say, **"Fill out the blanks at the bottom of the page. How did the numbers look? How does your head feel? How do your eyes feel? Do not worry about spelling."**

If you are testing a whole class of nonwriters, it is best to have two additional people to help write students' answers. Have children whisper their answers to the adults. Do not ask young children the questions out loud if there is more than one child, or all the answers will be the same.

Scoring: Count how many numbers the child copied in the different parts. Count the number of lines completed in all parts. Compare the students' results to the test norms below to see how much work should have been completed. Norms were established by averaging the "Highly Efficient Students'" scores. By dividing this number into your child's score, you will find the percent efficiency in each of the areas.

A functional vision problem exists if:

1. A child reports symptoms. The problem is severe if the child reports that his/her head hurts, his/her eyes hurt or burn, s/he feels dizzy or has similar symptoms. Even if a child reports minor symptoms such as being sleepy or tired, it is possible to help the child.

2. A child does not do the amount of work established by the norms.

3. A child has his/her head closer than 8 inches to the paper or tilts his/her head while working. The reason a person does this is to suppress the vision in one eye and thereby avoid symptoms.

Performance-based Vision Stress Test Norms: By averaging the "Highly Efficient Students'" scores, norms were established. By dividing this number into your child's score, you will find percent efficiency in each of the areas.

Grade	Age	Near-Far #-letters Parts A/E	Saccadic #-lines Parts C/F	Prolonged Test #-lines 5 - 10 minutes
K	5	11/15	3/4	16 20
1	6	16/20	4/5	18 34
2	7	33/36	5/5	20 38
3	8	37/39	6/7	24 44

Test Description: Fourth Grade to Adult

The test is divided into three parts: (1) near-far copy test: copying from chalkboard, (2) saccadic eye movement test: looking from word to word, and (3) prolonged eye teaming test: reading. These tests and charts may be copied for private use or the manual and test booklets may be purchased from the OEP Foundation (see Resources for the address). You will need a watch with a second hand or a stopwatch for giving the test.

The complete test must be given at one time. The child's eyes should be 14 inches from the test booklet (please adjust desk height). For young children, a kitchen table is too high. A card table is much better.

PART 1: Near-Far Copying.

A chart is placed on the wall. On the chart, letters appear in groups of three. The 20/20 charts come in two sizes: one for a distance of 10 feet; one for 20 feet. If you are testing an entire class, the larger charts are placed around the room so that each child can look directly at a chart 20 feet away. Students' desks are turned so that each student can see one of the charts 20 feet away. In one classroom you may have as many as 10 charts. In homes, the small chart is usually appropriate.

PART 1: Directions. Say, **"Open your test booklet and fill out the information at the top of the page. Name, grade, age and date. Do you have glasses? Where did you get them? Are you wearing them today?"** Next, say, **"Look at your paper. Put your finger on the 1 by the boxes under your name. I want you to copy as many of these letters as you can in one minute. Put three letters in each box. Go across the page. Does everyone know what you are going to do? Do not erase. On your mark, get set, go."** Time the students for one minute. Then say, **"Stop, put your pencils down."**

PART 2: Practice Saccadic Eye Movement - Looking From Word to Word.

This activity was designed to evaluate how efficiently a student can look from letter to letter to simulate the act of looking from word to word when reading. This is a practice section for activities in Parts 3, 4 and 6. Students will be working with letters. Letters are grouped to look similar to words in sentences.

Sample

scahyrs cdbe upomw dsxcsqyfgdvabk opfr hen

PART 2: Directions. Say, **"Look at the 2 on your paper. Part 2 is for practice. Notice what has been done. A line was drawn under the letters. Continue drawing this line, and when you come to the first A circle it. Go on to the first B and circle it. What will we do next? Right, we will go to the C and circle it. Does everyone get the idea? Let's practice and go until we get to Z."**

When everyone has completed this and understands the test say,

"Does anyone have any questions about what we are doing?"

PART 3: Directions for Saccadic Eye Movement

Say, **"Please turn the page. Put your finger on the number 3. Go as far as you can in one minute with the same activity you have been doing. Do as many lines as you can. Any questions? Start over with A each time you begin a new section. Do not erase. Ready, go."** After one minute say, **"Stop, turn to the next page."** Do not let the students rest their eyes. Keep them doing the same activity in Part 4.

PART 4: Directions for Prolonged Eye Teaming: Reading

Students will do the same activities they did in previous parts; at this stage for 15 minutes. With this activity we are evaluating eye alignment, binocularity, eye movement, focus, fusion, vergence and acuity under stress. This activity simulates reading but is much more difficult than actual reading because the student has to look at each letter. In order to compare amounts of work done in the first, second and third 5 minute time blocks, students will make a big X where they are working at the 5 minute time intervals.

PART 4: Directions. Say, **"We are going to keep doing the same activity. Look at the 4. Put your finger on the 4. You will start working there. Turn the page and look at the next pages. They are the same activity with the alphabet at the top of each page. You will do this activity until I say stop."** (Line 99 for sixth grade, line 172 for seventh grade and older.)

"Raise your hand if you need additional pages. Do not stop working. You will do the same thing you did in parts 2 and 3. We want to see how much work you can do in 15 minutes. When you have been working for 5 minutes and 10 minutes, I will tell you to mark a big X at the place you are working." (Show them about ½ inch with your fingers.) **"Make an X this big. Put your finger on the 4 again. We are ready to start the activity. Go as far as you can. Any questions? Do not erase. Ready, go."**

Record the starting time. Calculate 5, 10 and 15 minutes. Have the children mark an X on their papers at 5 and 10 minutes and stop the test after 15 minutes. While the children are doing this test, make notes on the test booklets of those children who get close to their work (8 inches or less), tilt their heads, rub their eyes, cover one eye, have watery eyes or squint. This is very important, because children get close to their work and tilt their heads so they can suppress the vision in one eye and thus avoid symptoms. These students usually have poor eye alignment.

At 5 minutes say, **"Mark an X."**

At 10 minutes say, **"Mark an X."**

At 15 minutes say, **"Stop."**

PART 5: Near-Far Copying: Fatigue Check

Part 5 is the same as Part 1. Students copy as many letters as they can in 1 minute. This is to see if there is a fatigue factor. Say, **"Put your finger on the 5. I want you to copy as many of these letters as you can in 1 minute. Put three letters in each box. Go across the page. This is the same activity that you did in Part A. Does everyone know what you are going to do? Do not erase. On your mark, get set, go."** Time the students for 1 minute. Then say, **"Stop, put your pencils down."**

PART 6: Saccadic Eye Movement: Fatigue Check.

This part is the same as Part 3. This section evaluates how many lines of work students can do in 1 minute after having used their eyes for about 20 minutes. Did any students have a fatigue factor?

Part 6: Directions. Say, **"Put your finger on the 6. Students, you will do the same thing you did in Parts 2, 3 and 4 for 1 minute. Do not erase. Do as many lines as you can. Any questions? Ready, go."** Time the students for 1 minute. **"Stop."**

Immediately after students finish the test: Say, **"Fill out the blanks at the bottom of the page. How does your head feel? How do your eyes feel? How did the letters look? Do not worry about spelling."**

Scoring: Count the number of letters the student copied in parts 1 and 5. Count the number of lines completed in parts 3, 4 and 6. Compare the students results to the following chart to see how much work should have been completed. Norms were established by averaging the "Highly Efficient Students" scores. By dividing this number into the student's score you will have percent efficiency in each of the areas.

A functional vision problem exists if:

1. A child reports symptoms. The problem is severe if the child reports that his/her head hurts, his/her eyes hurt or burn, s/he feels dizzy or has similar symptoms. Even if a child reports minor symptoms such as being sleepy or tired, it is possible to help the child with the above activities.

2. A child does not do the established amount of work.

3. A child has her/his head closer than 8 inches to the paper or tilts her/his head while working. (The reason a person does this is to suppress the vision in one eye and thereby avoid symptoms.)

4. A student gets lost going through the alphabet, skips lines or erases a lot.

Performance-based Vision Stress Test Norms: By averaging the "Highly Efficient Students'" scores, norms were established. By dividing this number into your child's score you will arrive at the percent efficiency in each of the areas.

Grade	Age	Near-Far #-letters Part 1/5	Saccadic #-lines Part 3/6	Prolonged Test #-lines 5 - 10 - 15 minutes
4	9	41/48	7/8	26 56
5	10	69/69	8/9	29 58 90
6	11	70/72	9/10	34 66 99
7	12	75/75	10/11	37 68 102
8	13	75/88	10/12	40 80 122
9	14	75/91	10/13	42 84 128
10	15	75/95	10/13	46 95 139
11	16	75/97	10/13+	48 97 143
12	17	75/99	10/13+	50 99 147

Chart for Use at 10'
K to Third Grade

154 213 354 415 523 131

221 351 453 541 154 213

354 415 523 131 221 351

441 543 124 232 342 424

512 132 234 332 432 524

Chart for Use at 10'
Fourth Grade to Adult

AVC BVT CRX DLA ETF

FJL GMH HUL ICW JRV

KNE LOU MVC NOR OYW

PLK QVC RLK SCT TIO

UCR VHC WRL XNK YEY

Chart for Use at 20'
K to Third Grade

154 213 354 415 523 131

221 351 453 541 154 213

354 415 523 131 221 351

441 543 124 232 342 424

512 132 234 332 432 524

Chart for Use at 20'
Fourth Grade to Adult

AVC BVT CRX DLA ETF

FJL GMH HUL ICW JRV

KNE LOU MVC NOR OYW

PLK QVC RLK SCT TIO

UCR VHC WRL XNK YEY

Performance-based Vision Stress Test
Kindergarten and First Grade

Name____________________________________ Grade ______ Age_______ Date__________

Glasses Y/N) ______________________Who from ______________Wearing today ____________

A

B

1 2 3 4 5

31 454 415 152 142 5213 215 523 2341 24 235

542 542 213 432 543 213 352 243 121 235 435

243 34 214 543 132 214 215 543 214 321 2451

231 141 545 214 131 125 521 132 142 214 523

452 314 451 124 542 231 253 321 254 252 253

45 214 251 142 215 243 215 512 232 242 1251

154 34 43 12 145 121 154 243 152 315 24 145

523 32 134 214 541 214 212 123 542 213 2135

____STOP __________

C

Test 1 2 3 4 5

23 431 314 532 124 452 213 421 214 435 4512 a

452 143 435 5312 1245 452 325 132 415 421 3 b

214 542 124 521 315 325 512 213 324 213 452 c

541 131 345 541 121 1 242 451 231 234 124 5 d

35 245 314 121 245 21 214 321 532 134 215 3 e

514 345 532 43 521 325 125 541 132 254 3451 f

243 24 542 2 314 54 53 432 452 213 3154 235 g

321 345 54 431 321 541 132 214 31 214 421 5 h

154 34 43 12 145 121 154 243 152 315 24 145 i

34 231 154 34 132 214 541 214 243 213 43 52 j

324 325 453 23 41 143 142 131 41 321 42 152 k

321 415 341 151 451 131 325 412 134 242 345 l

34 245 53 351 131 154 452 214 215 54 325 45 m

231 142 125 54 215 451 215 523 215 534 3541 n

215 54 341 214 2542 214 541 253 325 3143 35 o

234 2 51 134 152 124 251 152 124 243 314 45 p

45 214 251 142 215 243 215 512 232 242 1251 q

D

1 2 3 4 5

215 341 54 453 314 135 543 13 124 231 243 5 a

214 34 54 121 451 142 245 54 213 231 242 45 b

345 54 435 32 214 541 132 241 541 543 142 5 c

254 3122 214 54 512 254 421 135 321 325 452 d

321 415 341 151 451 131 325 412 134 242 345 e

34 245 53 351 131 154 452 214 215 54 325 45 f

231 142 125 54 215 451 215 523 215 534 3541 g

215 54 341 214 2542 214 541 253 325 3143 35 h

234 2 51 134 152 124 251 152 124 243 314 45 i

45 214 251 142 215 243 215 512 232 242 1251 j

154 34 43 12 145 121 154 243 152 315 24 145 k

34 231 154 34 132 214 541 214 243 213 43 52 l

324 325 453 23 41 143 142 131 41 321 42 152 m

321 415 341 151 451 131 325 412 134 242 345 n

34 245 53 351 131 154 452 214 215 54 325 45 o

231 142 125 54 215 451 215 523 215 534 3541 p

215 54 341 214 2542 214 541 253 325 3143 35 q

234 2 51 134 152 124 251 152 124 243 314 45 r

45 214 251 142 215 243 215 512 232 242 1251 s

154 34 43 12 145 121 154 243 152 315 24 145 t

1 2 3 4 5

34 231 154 34 132 214 541 214 243 213 43 52 u

324 325 453 23 41 143 142 131 41 321 42 152 v

321 415 341 151 451 131 325 412 134 242 345 w

34 245 53 351 131 154 452 214 215 54 325 45 x

231 142 125 54 215 451 215 523 215 534 3541 y

215 54 341 214 2542 214 541 253 325 3143 35 z

234 2 51 134 152 124 251 152 124 243 314 45 A

45 214 251 142 215 243 215 512 232 242 1251 B

154 34 43 12 145 121 154 243 152 315 24 145 C

34 231 154 34 132 214 541 214 243 213 43 52 D

324 325 453 23 41 143 142 131 41 321 42 152 E

321 415 341 151 451 131 325 412 134 242 345 F

34 245 53 351 131 154 452 214 215 54 325 45 G

231 142 125 54 215 451 215 523 215 534 3541 H

321 415 341 151 451 131 325 412 134 242 345 I

34 245 53 351 131 154 452 214 215 54 325 45 J

231 142 125 54 215 451 215 523 215 534 3541 K

215 54 341 214 2542 214 541 253 325 3143 35 L

234 2 51 134 152 124 251 152 124 243 314 45 M

45 214 251 142 215 243 215 512 232 242 1251 N

1 2 3 4 5

154 34 43 12 145 121 154 243 152 315 24 145 O

34 231 154 34 132 214 541 214 243 213 43 52 P

324 325 453 23 41 143 142 131 41 321 42 152 Q

321 415 341 151 451 131 325 412 134 242 345 R

34 245 53 351 131 154 452 214 215 54 325 45 S

231 142 125 54 215 451 215 523 215 534 3541 T

215 54 341 214 2542 214 541 253 325 3143 35 U

234 2 51 134 152 124 251 152 124 243 314 45 V

45 214 251 142 215 243 215 512 232 242 1251 W

154 34 43 12 145 121 154 243 152 315 24 145 X

34 231 154 34 132 214 541 214 243 213 43 52 Y

324 325 453 23 41 143 142 131 41 321 42 152 Z

451 341 54 453 314 135 543 13 124 231 243 5 a

413 34 54 121 451 142 245 54 213 231 242 45 b

435 54 435 32 214 541 132 241 541 543 142 5 c

254 3122 214 54 512 254 421 135 321 325 452 d

213 415 341 151 451 131 325 412 134 242 345 e

54 245 53 351 131 154 452 214 215 54 325 45 f

231 142 125 54 215 451 215 523 215 534 3541 g

E

F

1 2 3 4 5

215 54 341 214 2542 214 541 253 325 3143 35 a

234 2 51 134 152 124 251 152 124 243 314 45 b

45 214 251 142 215 243 215 512 232 242 1251 c

34 245 53 351 131 154 452 214 215 54 325 45 d

254 3122 214 54 512 254 421 135 321 325 452 e

154 34 43 12 145 121 154 243 152 315 24 145 f

34 231 154 34 132 214 541 214 243 213 43 52 g

231 142 125 54 215 451 215 523 215 534 3541 h

215 54 341 214 2542 214 541 253 325 3143 35 i

34 231 154 34 132 214 541 214 243 213 43 52 j

324 325 453 23 41 143 142 131 41 321 42 152 k

413 34 54 121 451 142 245 54 213 231 242 45 l

Head Feels?________________________________ Eyes Feel: ___________________________

Numbers Looked?____________________________

Performance-based Vision Stress Test
Grades 2 and 3
or Non-English speaking

Name____ Grade _______ Age________ Date__________

Glasses Y/N) _________________________Who from _______________Wearing today _____________

A

B

PRACTICE 1 2 3 4 5

342 32 425 131 543 432 214 215 154 213 215 131 34 235 5

341 314 541 543 314 31 342 124 2145 543 214 342 321 354

321 314 54 541 314 412 542 125 1245 213 2 34 321 235 45

235 31 141 145 54 534 341 125 543 231 31 215 21 124 254

143 542 121 154 451 214 125 541 131 535 432 213 242 235

341 314 541 543 314 31 342 124 2145 543 214 342 321 354

321 314 54 541 314 412 542 125 1245 213 2 34 321 235 45

235 31 141 145 54 534 341 125 543 231 31 215 21 124 254

34 341 531 412 254 215 425 231 152 12 532 324 24 251 15

32 45 342 321 145 341 543 32 124 541 131 253 342 143 54

____STOP_____________

1 2 3 4 5

C

One minute

542 231 245 542 121 154 543 213 325 515 542 123 232 543 a
231 214 542 215 154 524 232 215 512 1235 124 324 2345 5 b
153 435 541 154 345 434 132 214 243 125 32 215 241 1353 c
23 432 545 541 131 414 453 132 412 532 213 242 132 4351 d
23 454 324 231 154 342 143 124 243 124 321 121 132 2453 e
534 2435 532 231 135 431 154 432 142 425 351 125 341 45 f
23 345 53 325 4352 134 121 154 2425 243 142 231 422 325 g
342 231 245 542 121 154 543 213 325 515 542 123 232 543 h
431 214 542 215 154 524 232 215 512 1235 124 324 2345 5 i
353 435 541 154 345 434 132 214 243 125 32 215 241 1353 j
25 432 545 541 131 414 453 132 412 532 213 242 132 4351 k
534 2435 532 231 135 431 154 432 142 425 351 125 341 45 l
23 345 53 325 4352 134 121 154 2425 243 142 231 422 325 m
231 214 542 215 154 524 232 215 512 1235 124 324 2345 5 n
153 435 541 154 345 434 132 214 243 125 32 215 241 1353 o
23 432 545 541 131 214 453 132 412 532 213 242 132 4351 p
23 454 324 231 154 342 143 123 243 124 321 121 132 2453 q
534 2435 532 231 135 431 154 432 142 425 351 125 341 45 r
23 345 53 325 4352 134 121 154 2425 243 142 231 422 325 s
342 231 245 543 121 154 543 213 325 515 542 123 232 543 t
235 31 142 145 54 532 322 124 243 231 31 215 21 124 254 u
143 542 121 154 451 214 125 541 131 535 432 213 243 235 v
341 314 541 543 314 31 342 124 2145 543 214 342 321 354 w
534 2435 132 231 135 431 124 432 142 424 351 125 341 45 x
23 345 53 325 4152 133 121 154 2425 242 142 231 422 325 y
231 214 542 215 154 124 232 215 512 1235 124 324 2345 5 z

1 2 3 4 5

D

434 2435 532 231 135 431 154 432 142 425 351 125 341 45 a
43 345 53 325 4352 134 121 154 2425 243 142 231 422 325 b
345 231 245 542 121 154 543 213 325 515 542 123 232 543 c
421 214 542 215 154 524 232 215 512 1235 124 324 2345 5 d
253 435 541 154 345 434 132 214 243 125 32 215 241 1353 e
24 432 545 541 131 414 453 132 412 532 213 242 132 4351 f
234 214 542 215 154 524 232 215 512 1235 124 324 2345 5 g
154 435 541 154 345 434 132 214 243 125 32 215 241 1353 h
25 432 545 541 131 414 453 132 412 532 213 242 132 4351 i
34 454 324 231 154 342 143 124 243 124 321 121 132 2453 j
235 2435 532 231 135 431 154 432 142 425 351 125 341 45 k
25 345 53 325 4352 134 121 154 2425 243 142 231 422 325 l
242 231 245 542 121 154 543 213 325 515 542 123 232 543 m
531 214 542 215 154 524 232 215 512 1235 124 324 2345 5 n
453 435 541 154 345 434 132 214 243 125 32 215 241 1353 o
42 432 545 541 131 414 453 132 412 532 213 242 132 4351 p
32 431 545 541 131 414 453 134 412 532 213 242 132 4351 q
43 454 324 231 154 342 143 124 243 124 321 121 132 2453 r
234 2435 532 231 135 431 154 432 142 425 351 125 341 45 s
35 545 53 325 4352 134 121 154 2425 243 142 231 422 325 t
342 231 245 542 121 154 543 213 325 515 542 123 232 543 u
451 214 542 215 154 524 232 215 512 1235 124 324 2345 5 v
253 435 541 154 345 434 132 214 243 125 32 215 241 1353 w
42 432 545 541 131 414 453 132 412 532 213 242 132 4351 x
234 2435 532 231 135 431 154 432 142 425 351 125 341 45 y
43 345 53 325 4352 134 121 154 2425 243 142 231 422 325 z

1 2 3 4 5

542 231 245 542 121 154 543 213 325 515 542 123 232 543 a
45 432 545 541 131 414 453 132 412 532 213 242 132 4351 b
34 454 324 231 154 342 143 124 243 124 321 121 132 2453 c
245 2435 532 231 135 431 154 432 142 425 351 125 341 45 d
43 545 53 325 4352 134 121 154 2425 243 142 231 422 325 e
532 231 245 542 121 154 543 213 325 515 542 123 232 543 f
341 214 542 215 154 524 232 215 512 1235 124 324 2345 5 g
252 435 541 154 345 434 132 214 243 125 32 215 241 1353 h
34 432 545 541 131 414 453 132 412 532 213 242 132 4351 i
325 231 245 542 121 154 543 213 325 515 542 123 232 543 j
531 214 542 215 154 524 232 215 512 1235 124 324 2345 5 k
425 435 541 154 345 434 132 214 243 125 32 215 241 1353 l
23 432 545 541 131 414 453 132 412 532 213 242 132 4351 m
253 214 542 215 154 524 232 215 512 1235 124 324 2345 5 n
135 435 541 154 345 434 132 214 243 125 32 215 241 1353 o
54 432 545 541 131 414 453 132 412 532 213 242 132 4351 p
53 454 324 231 154 342 143 124 243 124 321 121 132 2453 q
252 2435 532 231 135 431 154 432 142 425 351 125 341 45 r
23 345 53 325 4352 134 121 154 2425 243 142 231 422 325 s
34 545 53 325 4352 134 121 154 2425 243 142 231 422 325 t
542 231 245 542 121 154 543 213 325 515 542 123 232 543 u
251 214 542 215 154 524 232 215 512 1235 124 324 2345 5 v
453 435 541 154 345 434 132 214 243 125 32 215 241 1353 w
34 432 545 541 131 414 453 132 412 532 213 242 132 4351 x
253 2435 532 231 135 431 154 432 142 425 351 125 341 45 y
52 345 53 325 4352 134 121 154 2425 243 142 231 422 325 z

1 2 3 4 5

231 245 542 121 154 543 213 325 515 542 123 232 323 543 a

52 231 245 542 121 154 543 213 325 515 542 123 232 543 b

434 2435 532 231 135 431 154 432 142 425 351 125 341 45 c

52 345 53 325 4352 134 121 154 2425 243 142 231 422 325 d

543 231 245 542 121 154 543 213 325 515 542 123 232 543 e

421 214 542 215 154 524 232 215 512 1235 124 324 2345 5 f

453 435 541 154 345 434 132 214 243 125 32 215 241 1353 g

42 432 545 541 131 414 453 132 412 532 213 242 132 4351 h

523 2435 532 231 135 431 154 432 54 142 425 351 125 341 45 i

34 345 53 325 4352 134 121 154 2425 243 142 231 422 325 j

435 231 245 542 121 154 543 213 325 515 542 123 232 543 k

534 214 542 215 154 524 232 215 512 1235 124 324 2345 5 l

524 435 541 154 345 434 132 214 243 125 32 215 241 1353 m

35 432 545 541 131 414 453 132 412 532 213 242 132 4351 n

432 214 542 215 154 524 232 215 512 1235 124 324 2345 5 o

314 435 541 154 345 434 132 214 243 125 32 215 241 1353 p

32 432 545 541 131 414 453 132 412 532 213 242 132 4351 q

53 454 324 231 154 342 143 124 243 124 321 121 132 2453 r

45 432 545 541 131 414 453 132 412 532 213 242 132 4351 s

243 214 542 215 154 524 232 215 512 1235 124 324 2345 5 t

413 435 541 154 345 434 132 214 243 125 32 215 241 1353 u

32 432 545 541 131 414 453 132 412 532 213 242 132 4351 v

233 54 324 231 154 342 143 124 243 124 321 121 132 2453 w

254 2435 532 231 135 431 154 432 142 425 351 125 341 45 x

243 45 53 325 4352 134 121 154 2425 243 142 231 422 325 y

532 32 53 325 4352 134 121 154 2425 243 142 231 422 325 z

E

F

One minute 1 2 3 4 5

434 2435 532 231 135 431 154 432 142 425 351 125 341 45 a
43 345 53 325 4352 134 121 154 2425 243 142 231 422 325 b
345 231 245 542 121 154 543 213 325 515 542 123 232 543 c
421 214 542 215 154 524 232 215 512 1235 124 324 2345 5 d
253 435 541 154 345 434 132 214 243 125 32 215 241 1353 e
44 432 545 541 131 414 453 132 412 532 213 242 132 4351 f
234 214 542 215 154 524 232 215 512 1235 124 324 2345 5 g
154 435 541 154 345 434 132 214 243 125 32 215 241 1353 h
25 432 545 541 131 414 453 132 412 532 213 242 132 4351 i
34 454 324 231 154 342 143 124 243 124 321 121 132 2453 j
235 2435 532 231 135 431 154 432 142 425 351 125 341 45 k
25 345 53 325 4352 134 121 154 2425 243 142 231 422 325 l
242 231 245 542 121 154 543 213 325 515 542 123 232 543 m
531 214 542 215 154 524 232 215 512 1235 124 324 2345 5 n
434 2435 532 231 135 431 154 432 142 425 351 125 341 45 o
52 345 53 325 4352 134 121 154 2425 243 142 231 422 325 p
543 231 245 542 121 154 543 213 325 515 542 123 232 543 q

Head Feels?________________________Eyes Feel: ________________________

Numbers Looked?________________________

Performance-based Vision Stress Test
Grades 4 to Adult

Name____________________________________ Grade ______ Age_______ Date_________

Glasses Y/N) ______________________Who from ______________Wearing today ____________

1

a b c d e f g h i j k l m n o p q r s t u v w x y z

2

Practice

bnt rey nj cal nic juy cas swe mip olp kio lip nmo ble
bhn wrtv vby ext hav cety hnr pwx chw hpwd myp imk di
nqs rtw nd pim ngt ytlr wxc rey mupc htez wxe mipe nup
hec sty vfy mup wcf hyen mjl km jgt hw pljue ce gnei
zec efi hjnop lew hec vce tyu mop lmb vbc dei w rty iu
muy bcv iuo swe ikn yjn xsdj ldn ud sert wke rty uks vb
awe drf ntr mlr tew celm nrel vne mew zxtme wec vmne
xrtn xtwp ctyu bnut wrc ctv bon vctr hnt lmbn xt rotg
vtn ctop rctp xtyx cty opc pq vt cwed wqn opq svb dru
isr xzt vrn idc xtsu nuk kls dsri plsn pltm nrs bvip
rten zxw rwtn mwtp bvo puml numy buw hubc zwvn mbvt
kuwt lrtw nptx ctv pul xct pql mnx uycr mzy ctw dyzw

___________________________________STOP____________

3

a b c d e f g h i j k l m n o p q r s t u v w x y z

vop zwy cak gaxz pwd oumac dwbn mqr tbp zew qum nbh pe gxf 1
pqx nbr uncm vxyp xzy uij hdq cpr wer tun mcod p dqu pmkl 2
lmfw qrxs ahfk luy sfew zunp rhfn bgre dcm w omgbf exc trx 3
bghr unmk lfr fhvea sedhn pleix wuy tho vxc rivn meiw qmn 4
bvjr ynmx wme pjh vcx zpwj wzxkn mp rect pim nkd xwe rkn 5
vlwe ecln zopn vbt yew saflh wcm pum ced rcnh wec ven bxu 6
punc wxukn wxi meno iex ahg hcr bcie yiom tpq xok lpuy twq 7
scpk pqrw xvx nmeq knir pq tnc hrp nrop xwvr spwx upm nik 8
fsx chwsn pewu ptoc nrx arnt wq m stpj nyv wec puxz wun mx 9
byus tr edc sie kln brew cwvb pun xrvt lme zpiv rtv ewt op 10
nipw uth nwb peg cre momw tzxs pli mbep rxop sxmn pw zrtu 11
unmk lplw rysa puhn xwrt htyn xprtx cetr rpx tebm pmun zo 12

---

nuy hty rav ced pol gaw wef mopb von wey lob liuj jub 13
ubr nvpb wrtx dxcg pok lmy wer xcy vyn oclg zaw hdm ok 14
das fxi puk mny xadh ner unmr wtynv ceo pmen xdw cfh w 15
xcu jtf pws xmbf pwex wxz dgu npk lwmg esx cet ugm re 16
wnhe lm xew bhn whtc jlop uk egtih wec xth mic cdf ivj 17
swer tfg sxd dju btyn ipjl csk mwr pre dkr wxc mkrt r 18
awe drf gtr mlr tew celb nrel vne mew zxtme wec vmne 19
xrtn xtwp ctyu bnut wrc ctv bon vctr hnt lmbn xt rotg 20
vtn ctop rctp xtyx cty opc pq vt cwed wqn opq svb dru 21
plm try cery poms cey qspm gsm brt wey ve dse fto pm 22
vetm heu cty gpm dpb num wump rbv bcvt plk jhy rvy vyw 23
crot frmw eyvt pvxr moyc nzxpl ct pvxy lzn cewy wx mzo 24

4

a b c d e f g h i j k l m n o p q r s t u v w x y z

sdea poly nec nead swda mvc hup bdf hrt jbu pub xze rty 1
xec n sxa wry vhc hpo ncg erd hyx chy sdu hynhd sdbv nbg 2
huep nmoe vbce vh hft pllef xwe tyrf cthg mui plk vgn po 3
d dcv mph klx dhw cxf tnv vbt sce rty uio pol cvn nix ty 4
weg ynh wlic v bnip lui klmj dfj es cef hjmk cgft nbn z 5
wek wnk cedkp vnil vetl cdr hy puv bg acet vc ghf hu vab 6
t net vyt bnh umwe vbt klw wex cer mju grt nix cty cvmn 7
vb norw nwr vcx uym nir erw qoc xbn mwp vnr rom cor pre 8
wec vdp vbn iupm gpr vbpq vb pqcn vet pow mn ery vcir p 9
cde frt hnt yru detr cd ghys mupm syn mnu banv stm pom 10
sbr pmtn whtx wnmth mnuc xty puabn rtyu mnwu cbluv xasy 11
myuv cvt xtu plwj hgn cvuw rtn czt plik mxba nhj fxh r 12
hyr sfd cxy nbt hbar rvw xc cvh nbr xwp tym nmp xze dz 13

---

cdep jh hye acd ghr tep wes das meaf hnb hnp mgb aset 14
ghrt dasb kcs far hgec pfnc qwzx opnc hsdr hyw hdf mp 15
hpdm rtoec hiu wiep wxc lkje dhf nbf cxv bedf phr egq 16
wxu mpm edgu guyc whp yhn exci mipl bghil wex cef pj 17
djc grh kju cft vyj dks xvb hlp xce nlpky bhky xdf rt 18
vrt jikp vkly hlyb vhlw vnmw rty pmf vmr vnt hty unp 19
xce pngh hor gth yto vet tob vrpy hec vpt cbp xcy pqc 20
vty weq nmt nqx cet xrt yip mir cavb bry xsr yws nmo p 21
pst nuc dft hup dewt pmn xgt erw uy bnr rmup wedu bnre 22
nyu chr bgvt htwe sfrev pumn gvlk cbv vcbt rwen bc cn 23
ndcw cnhy tunw pokm nmjwv ecf hgt cexp ouq hxv ntu bu 24
wch ctt chu nhg fgw rxv ghyt rtw sedcy mun pumz xty z 25

a b c d e f g h i j k l m n o p q r s t u v w x y z

wty bov cde dar pim opr ecay pmn cwas mgv cep vbw pnx 26

ubr nvpb wrtx dxcg pok lmy wer xcy vyn oclg zaw hdm ok 27

das fxi puk mny xadh ner unmr wtynv ceo pmen xdw cfh w 28

xcu jtf pws xmbf pwex wxz dgu npk lwmg esx cet ugm re 29

wnhe lm xew bhn whtc jlop uk egtih wec xth mic cdf ivj 30

swer tfg sxd dju btyn ipjl csk mwr pre dkr wxc mkrt r 31

awe drf gtr mlr tew celb nrel vne mew zxtme wec vmne 32

xrtn xtwp ctyu bnut wrc ctv bon vctr hnt lmbn xt rotg 33

vtn ctop rctp xtyx cty opc pq vt cwed wqn opq svb dru 34

isr xzt vrn sdc xtsu tk kuls dsri plsu pltm nrs bvip 35

rven zxw rwtn mwtp bvo puml numy buw hubc zwvn mbvt 36

mopv mpnw crot frmw ewvt pvxr mopc nzxpl ct pvxc lmn 37

cewy wxrn mqpo cey mopr xewc bny moui lmry xewc vez 38

---

veth hnt vex samt rec mray poma mvbh haxe expt nupi 39

bhn wrtv vby ext hav cety hnr pwx chw hpwd myp imk di 40

nqs rtw nd pim ngt ytlr wxc rey mupc htez wxe mipe nup 41

hec sty vfy mup wcf hyen mjl km jgt hw pljue ce gnei 42

zec efi hjnop lew hec vce tyu mop lmb vbc dei w rty iu 43

muy bcv iuo swe ikn yjn xsdj lmn md sert nke rty uks vb 44

qlx cvn wr tru clp xctl xce nkmw erty ui vmp wovm cv 45

xrt env wrt vny pcv vnr yor vcy bno xzs rwe tuo dpc v 46

rtn uml kpm bup bnw rqp vnt cty xcp coqp pqo ctr xuru 47

plm try cery poms cey qspm gsm brt wey ve dse fto pm 48

vetm heu cty gpm dpb num wump rbv bcvt plk jhy rvy vyw 49

vuwt lrvw nptx ctv pul xct pql mnx uycr muy ctz mynz 50

a b c d e f g h i j k l m n o p q r s t u v w x y z

ytx brw opc dai cxw qu mae rte mov cxe rqw piy mnu bde 51
pom dasb kcs far hgec pfnc qwzx opnc hsdr hyw hdf mp 52
hpdm rtoec hiu wiep wxc lkje dhf nbf cxv bedf phr mnt 53
vce cxw opl egq wxu mpm edgu guyc whp yhn exc bvr numu 54
tc uji uy mopl bghei wex cnvr ewr dfs xsd asz zsj f pj 55
dec grh nke rty uks vb qlx cvn wr tru clp xctl xce nkmw 56
erty ui vmp wovm cv xrt env wrt vny pcv vnr yor vcy bno 57
xzs rwe tuo dpc v mtn uml kpm bup bnw rqp vnt cty xcp 58
coqp pqo ctr xuru plm try cery poms cey qspm gsm brt wey 59
ve dse vrn idc xtsu nuk kls dsri plvn pltm nrs bvip rten 60
zxw rwtn mwtp bvo puml numy bxuw hubc zwvn mbvt mxv mpnw 61
crot frmw eyvt pvxr moyc nzxpl ct pvxc lzn cewy wxrn mzo 62

---

oiuy rft ght wse sac nvc nie rty mnj ace fsd ambd dsa i 63
miw mwrtv vby ext hav cety hnr pwx chw hpwd myp imk di 64
nqs rew nd pim ngt ytlr wxc rey mupc htez wxe fipe nup 65
hec sty vfg mup wcf hyen mjl gm jyt hw pljue ce ghe mo 66
zec efi hjnop lew hec vie tyu mop lmb vbc dei w rty ju 67
sjer tfg skd dju btyn ipjl csk mwr pre dkr wxc mkrl r 68
awe drf gtr mlr tew celb nrel vne mew zxtme wec vmne 69
xrtn xtwp coyu bnut wrc ctv bon vctr hnp lmbn xp rotg 70
rtn uml kpm bup bnw rqp vnt cty xcp coqp pqo ctr xuru 71
plm try cery poms cey qspm gsm brt wey ve dse fto pm 72
vetm heu cty gpm dpb num wump rbv bcvt plk jhy rvy vyw 73
nuwt lrtw nptx ctv pul xct pql mnx uycr muy ctw cynz 74

a b c d e f g h i j k l m n o p q r s t u v w x y z

vur nb mic xda npn lkl avx nju bxd ewz skl nvg gfd bdeg	75
pom dasb kcs far hgec pfnc qwzx opnc hsdr hyw hdf mp	76
hpdm rtoec hiu wiep wxc lkje dhf nbf cxv bedf phr mnt	77
vce cxw opl egq wxu mpm edgu guyc whp yhn exc bvr numu	78
tc uji uy mopl bghei wex cnvr ewr dfs xsd asz zsj f pj	79
swer tfg sxd dju btyn ipjl csk mwr pre dkr wxc mkrt r	80
awe drf gtr mlr tew celb nrel vne mew zxtme wec vmne	81
xrtn xtwp ctyu bnut wrc ctv bon vctr hnt lmbn xt rotg	82
vtn ctop rctp xtyx cty opc pq vt cwed wqn opq svb dru	83
cde frt hnt yru detr cd ghys mupm syn mnu banv stm pom	84
sbr pmtn whtx wnmth mnuc xty puabn rtyu mnwu cbluv xasy	85
myuv cvt xtu plwj hgn cvuw rtn czt plik mxba nhj fxh r	86
wch ctt chu nhg fgw rxv ghyt rtw sedcy mun pumz xty z	87

---

bnt rey nj cal nic juy cas swe mip olp kio lip nmo bde	88
bhn wrtv vby ext hav cety hnr pwx chw hpwd myp imk di	89
nqs rtw nd pim ngt ytlr wxc rey mupc htez wxe mipe nup	90
hec sty vfy mup wcf hyen mgl km jgt hw pljue ce gnei	91
zec efi hjnop lew hec vce tju mop lmb vbc dei wk ty iu	92
muy bcv iuo swe ikn yjn xsdj lam md selt nke rmy uks vb	93
awe drf gtr mlr tew celb nrel vne mew zxtme wec vmne	94
xrtn xtwp ctyu bnut wrc ctv bon vctr hnt lmbn xt rotg	95
vtn ctop rctp xtyx cty opc pq vt cwed wqn opq svb dru	96
isr xzt vrn idc xtsu nuk kls dsri plsn pltm nrs bvip	97
rten zxw rwtn mwtp bvo puml numy buw hubc zwvn mbvt	98
kuwt lrtw nptx ctv pul xct pql mnx uycr mzy ctw dyzw	99

a b c d e f g h i j k l m n o p q r s t u v w x y z

nuy hty rav ced pol gaw wef mopb von wey lob liuj jub 100

ubr nvpb wrtx dxcg pok lmy wer xcy vyn oclg zaw hdm ok 101

das fxi puk mny xadh ner unmr wtynv ceo pmen xdw cfh w 102

xcu jtf pws xmbf pwex wxz dgu npk lwmg esx cet ugm re 103

wnhe lm xew bhn whtc jlop uk egtih wec xth mic cdf ivj 104

swer tfg sxd dju btyn ipjl csk mwr pre dkr wxc mkrt r 105

vewe drf gtr mlr tew celb nrel vne mew zxtme wec vmne 106

xrtn xtwp ctyu bnut wrc ctv bon vctr hnt lmbn xt rotg 107

vtn ctop rctp xtyx cty opc pq vt cwed wqn opq svb dru 108

plm try cery poms cey qspm gsm brt wey ve dse fto pm 109

vetm heu cty gpm dpb num wump rbv bcvt plk jhy rvy vyw 110

crot frmw eyvt pvxr moyc nyxpl ct pvxy lzn cewy wx mzo 111

---

cae tyr rwe kio nma nbe iopl kjmn xdes wety xsa vbs p 112

bhn wrtv vby ext hav cety hnr pwx chw hpwd myp imk di 113

nqs rtw nd pim ngt ytlr wxc rey mupc htez wxe mipe nup 114

hec sty vfy mup wcf hyen mjl km jgt hw pljue ce gnei 115

zec efi hjnop lew hec vce tyu mop lmb vbc dei w rty iu 116

swer tfg sxd dju btyn ipjl csk mwr pre dkr wxc mkrt r 117

awe drf gtr mlr tew celb nrel vne mew zxtme wec vmne 118

xrtn xtwp ctyu bnut wrc ctv bon vctr hnt lmbn xt rotg 119

vtn ctop rctp xtyx cty opc pq vt cwed wqn opq svb dru 120

isr xsz vrn itds xtsu nuk ls dsri plsn pltm nrs bvip 121

rten zxw rwtn mwtp bvo puml numy buw hubc zwvn mbvt 122

nuwt lrtw nptx ctv pul xct pql mnx uycr muy ctw mzyr 123

a b c d e f g h i j k l m n o p q r s t u v w x y z

jio nb mic xda npn lkl avx nju bxd ewz skl nvg gfd bdeg 124
uyt dasb kcs far hgec pfnc qwzx opnc hsdr hyw hdf mp 125
hpdm rtoec hiu wiep wxc lkje dhf nbf cxv bedf phr mnt 126
vce cxw opl egq wxu mpm edgu guyc whp yhn exc bvr numu 127
tc uji uy mopl bghei wex cnvr ewr dfs xsd asz zsj f pj 128
swer tfg sxd dju btyn ipjl csk mwr pre dkr wxc mkrt r 129
awe drf gtr mlr tew celb nrel vne mew zxtme wec vmne 130
xrtn xtwp ctyu bnut wrc ctv bon vctr hnt lmbn xt rotg 131
vtn ctop rctp xtyx cty opc pq vt cwed wqn opq svb dru 132
cde frt hnt yru detr cd ghys mupm syn mnu banv stm pom 133
sbr pmtn whtx wnmth mnuc xty puabn rtyu mnwu cbluv xasy 134
myuv cvt xtu plwj hgn cvuw rtn czt plik mxba nhj fxh r 135
wch ctt chu nhg fgw rxv ghyt rtw sedcy mun pumz xty z 136

---

wef rey nj cal nic juy cas swe mip olp kio lip nmo bde 137
bhn wrtv vby ext hav cety hnr pwx chw hpwd myp imk di 138
nqs rtw nd pim ngt ytlr wxc rey mupc htez wxe mipe nup 139
hec sty vfy mup wcf hygn mjl km jgt hw pljhe ce gnei 140
zec efi hjnop lew hec vce tyu mjp lmb vbc dki w rty iu 141
muy bcv iuo swe ikn yjn xsdj lan md sert nke rtl uks vb 142
awe drf gtr mlr tew celb nrel vne mew zxtme wec vmne 143
xrtn xtwp ctyu bnut wrc ctv bon vctr hnt lmbn xt rotg 144
vtn cto rctp xtyx cty opc pq vt cwed wqn opq srvb dru 145
isr xzt vrn sdc xtsu tuk kls dsri plsn putm nrs bvip 146
rtvn zxw rwtn mwtp bvo puml numy buw hubc zwvn mbvt 147
muwt lrtw nptx ctv pul xct pql mnx uycr mzy ctw dyzw 148

a b c d e f g h i j k l m n o p q r s t u v w x y z

khn hty rav ced pol gaw wef mopb von wey lob liuj jub 149
ybr nvpb wrtx dxcg pok lmy wer xcy vyn oclg zaw hdm ok 150
xas fxi puk mny xadh ner unmr wtynv ceo pmen xdw cfh w 151
xcu jtf pws xmbf pwex wxz dgu npk lwmg esx cet ugm re 152
wnhe lm xew bhn whtc jlop uk egtih wec xth mic cdf ivj 153
swer tfg sxd dju btyn ipjl csk mwr pre dkr wxc mkrt r 154
awe drf gtr mlr tew celb nrel vne mew zxtme wec vmne 155
xrtn xtwp ctyu bnut wrc ctv bon vctr hnt lmbn xt rotg 156
vtn ctop rctp xtyx cty opc pq vt cwed wqn opq svb dru 157
plm try cery poms cey qspm gsm brt wey ve dse fto pm 158
vetm heu cty gpm dpb num wump rbv bcvt plk jhy rvy vyw 159
crot frmw eyvt pvxr moyc nzxpl ct pvxy lzn cewy wx mzo 160

---

wsv tyr rwe kio nma nbe iopl kjmn xdes wety xsa vbs p 161
xsn wrtb vby ext hav cety hnr pwx chw hpwd myp imk di 162
nqs rtw nd pim ngt ytlr wxc rey mupc htez wxe mipe nup 163
hec sty vfy mup wcf hygn mjl km jgt mw plhue ceh gnei 164
zec efi hjnop lew hec vce tyu mop lmb vbc dei w rty iu 165
swer tfg sxd dju btyn ipjl csk mwr pre dkr wxc mkrt r 166
awe drf gtr mlr tew celb nrel vne mew zxtme wec vmne 167
xrtn xtwp ctyu bnut wrc ctv bon vctr hnt lmbn xt rotg 168
vtn ctop rctp xtyx cty opc pq vt cwed wqn oprq vb dru 169
isr xzt vrn idc xtsu nuk kls dsri plsn pltm nrs bvip 170
rten zxw rwtn mwtp bvo puml numy buw hubc zwvn mbvt 171
nuwt lrtw nptx ctv pul xct pql mnx uycr muy ctw mzyr 172

5

6

a b c d e f g h i j k l m n o p q r s t u v w x y z

cwt nb mic xda npn lkl avx nju bxd ewz skl nvg gfd bdeg 1

pom dasb kcs far hgec pfnc qwzx opnc hsdr hyw hdf mp 2

hpdm rtoec hiu wiep wxc lkje dhf nbf cxv bedf phr mnt 3

vce cxw opl egq wxu mpm edgu guyc whp yhn exc bvr numu 4

tc uji uy mopl bghei wex cnvr ewr dfs xsd asz zsj f pj 5

swer tfg sxd dju btyn ipjl csk mwr pre dkr wxc mkrt r 6

awe drf gtr mlr tew celb nrel vne mew zxtme wec vmne 7

xrtn xtwp ctyu bnut wrc ctv bon vctr hnt lmbn xt rotg 8

vtn ctop rctp xtyx cty opc pq vt cwed wqn opq svb dru 9

cde frt hnt yru detr cd ghys mupm syn mnu banv stm pom 10

sbr pmtn whtx wnmth mnuc xty puabn rtyu mnwu cbluv xasy 11

myuv cvt xtu plwj hgn cvuw rtn czt plik mxba nhj fxh r 12

wch ctt chu nhg fgw rxv ghyt rtw sedcy mun pumz xty z 13

---

bnt rey nj cal nic juy cas swe mip olp kio lip nmo bde 14

bhn wrtv vby ext hav cety hnr pwx chw hpwd myp imk di 15

nqs rtw nd pim ngt ytlr wxc rey mupc htez wxe mipe nup 16

hec sty vfy mup wcf hyen mjl km jgt hw pljue ce gnei 17

tc uji uy mopl bghei wex cnvr ewr dfs xsd asz zsj f pj 18

swer tfg sxd dju btyn ipjl csk mwr pre dkr wxc mkrt r 19

Head Feels?________________ Eyes Feel: ________________

Letters Looked? ________________

About The Authors

Allen Crane received his bachelor of science degree in geology from Texas Technological College in 1951 and pursued a career as an oil geologist for many years. His scientific training taught him to question everything diligently—to look for answers in places no one else had looked.

In 1972, Mr. Crane received his master's degree in guidance and counseling from Western New Mexico University and began his career in education as an elementary counselor. He continued his education, acquiring more training through the Orton Society, University of Northern Colorado, University of New Mexico, New Mexico State University, Black Hills State College and the University of Wyoming, focusing on children's learning problems. Mr. Crane worked four years as a director of special education and fifteen years as a resource teacher. Mr. Crane was certified as a special education teacher, counselor, psychologist, and reading specialist.

While a resource teacher and Director of Title I at the Pine Ridge Indian Reservation at Pine Ridge, South Dakota, Mr. Crane became acutely aware of vision problems as a special component of learning difficulties. In search of solutions he visited colleges, clinics and practitioners across the nation. After retiring from teaching, he conducted vision training activities in clinics and schools under the guidance of seven optometrists. Mr. Crane collaborated with Dr. Bruce Wick in authoring the Crane-Wick Vision and Hearing Efficiency Test, now the Performance-based Vision Stress Test, and in developing *Vision Screening & Diagnostics,* a computer vision screening program. Mr. Crane normed and standardized (established how much visual work a highly efficient child could complete in a set amount of time) the Performance-based Vision Stress Test on over 2,000 children in six states.

During this process, Mr. Crane became aware of other factors relating to learning problems and began seeking answers in the areas of allergies, hearing and medicine. He does not believe in the diagnoses of dyslexia, learning disability, attention deficit disorder or attention deficit hyperactive disorder. Mr. Crane believes the answers lie in an inter-professional examination of the whole child, and that solutions to a child's problems are either medical, vision or a combination. **Further, he believes that his problem-solving approach can help over half of the children in any classroom become more efficient students; that means not just children with handicaps but half of *all* children.** This includes "good" students who instead of developing headaches and blurry vision can now comfortably read for pleasure. It also includes children who, after their problems have been corrected, have improved comprehension and take only 20 minutes to do an activity which previously took them an hour. Many of these students will make such dramatic progress that they will be moved out of special education, be symptom-free and turn in assignments on time. Their grades will improve from C, D and F to A, B and C.

Virginia Crane earned her bachelor of science degree from Phillips University in Enid, Oklahoma, in 1964. She worked as a dormitory supervisor in Navajo boarding schools and taught eighth grade American history and fourth grade before returning to school for an advanced degree. In 1970, she earned a guidance and counseling master's degree from Adams State College in

Alamosa, Colorado. She then worked for two years as an elementary counselor in Farmington, New Mexico, where she met and married Allen Crane.

Mrs. Crane received additional training in special education and counseling from the University of Northern Colorado, University of New Mexico, New Mexico State University, Black Hills State College and the University of Wyoming. She taught in special education classrooms for twenty-one years. During three of these years, the Cranes team-taught in the same classroom. Virginia retired from formal teaching in 1992. Mrs. Crane was certified as a special education teacher, teacher, counselor, and psychologist.

Index

Buzzards to Bluebirds outlines exactly how you can help your child realize her or his potential in six weeks. The authors, who team-taught for many years, dedicated three decades to researching and developing this valuable material. Part I is for parents, Part II is for the parent-teacher team, Part III is for schools. The book offers a clear guide to identifying then eliminating problems that trigger learning difficulties--from straightforward checklists, tests and charts, here are practical, proven ways to resolve learning and behavior problems.

"...the finest reading...about the problems faced by many students. The information and tests in **Buzzards to Bluebirds** will help parents readily address possible learning difficulties in an immediate and gratifying manner. A valuable resource."

D. R. Magill, Principal, Bayfield Elementary
Bayfield, Colorado

"...a broad yet succinct guide to therapies that may be of great help to your struggling child - new avenues for parents and educators who've felt that surely more could be done for their children."

K. Romney, M.D.
Wray, Colorado

"Empowering! **Buzzards to Bluebirds will** empower you, will empower parents. Allen and Virginia Crane have effectively looked for answers to the high rate of student failure in the classroom. Their research has resulted in the development of an effective method for easy, confident identification of how children learn and how to help bring any necessary changes and improvements."

John A. Thomas, O.D.,
Wheat Ridge, Colorado

Order Form for Buzzards to Bluebirds

To: Wolf Creek Endeavors
P.O. Box 242,
Wray, CO. 80758

Here's my check, payable to Wolf Creek Endeavors.
Please send the book(s) immediately.

Name: ______________________________

Address: ______________________________

City: ____________________ State: ______ Zip: ______

		Quantity	Cost
1 copy	$19.95		
2-11 copies	$16.00 each		
12-49 copies	$14.00 each		
50-99 copies	$12.00 each		
Over 100 copies	$10.00 each		

REMEMBER, for free shipping/handling, send payment with order.
Otherwise, for 1-11 books, add $3 for ship/handling; 12+ books add $8.